# BILL'S BOOK

## Memories of a Yorkshire Wolds Character

by

### Billy Harrison

Edited by

### Peter Halkon

HUTTON PRESS

1990

Published by the Hutton Press Ltd.
130 Canada Drive, Cherry Burton, Beverley
East Yorkshire HU17 7SB

Printed and bound by
Clifford Ward & Co. (Bridlington) Ltd.
55 West Street, Bridlington, East Yorkshire
YO15 3DZ

ISBN 0 907033 88 1

*Billy Harrison, photo courtesy of Mrs. M. Halkon*

# CONTENTS

# Preface

I first met Bill about ten years ago at the Gate Inn. Millington, one of his favourite haunts. I overheard him talking to Sefton Cottom, Head of Music at Pocklington School about his life at Nunburnholme, the village where he was born and bred, before the First World War. This particularly interested me as my parents had recently moved to Nunburnholme, and I was a newly appointed history teacher, eager for first hand accounts of this period.

Subsequently I was honoured to be among his wide circle of friends. I was captivated by his wit and perceptive comment about life early this century, which included work in the prestigious gardens at Warter Priory, going over the top at Cambrai in 1917 and steam threshing. I was also lucky enough to be among those entertai-ned by his musicianship on fiddle and cello, which he had played in country dance bands in the pre-television age.

In 1980 Bill allowed me to make some oral history recordings of his reminiscences. Following this and several visits to Bransholme High School, where he held large groups of children spell-bound by his story, he was finally persuaded to write this book, which originally filled eight exercise books. Painstakingly written in a small, neat hand, it covers a period from 1898 until 1942, when he moved to Millington. He rounded off the story shortly before his death in July 1986, at the age of eighty-eight.

In the small amount of editing that I have done, I have remained faithful as far as possible to Bill's original words and consequently have included his East Yorkshire dialect phonetical spellings in the quotations.

Bill died before we could discuss editing the book and I was unable to suggest which sections might benefit from expansion or the inclusion of greater detail. I have included other information in order to place Bill's story in a wider perspective, making it more meaningful for those not so familiar with the area around Nunburnholme. These sources include 'Nunburnholme, its history and antiquities.' by the Rev. M.C.F. Morris (London 1907), 'Yorkshire Reminiscences' (London 1922) by the same author, and newspaper and magazine articles from the Local Studies library in Hull Central Library. I am most grateful to the staff there for their help. For the chapters on the First World War, I consulted E. Wyrall's 'The West Yorkshire Regiment in the War 1914-18' (2 vols,

Bodley Head 1924 and 1927), 'The history of the 1/6th Battalion, the West Yorkshire Regiment' by E.V. Tempest (Lund Humphries 1921) and 'The history of the 2/6th Battalion, West Yorkshire Regiment' by E.C. Gregory (same publisher 1923). I am most grateful to the staff of the Prince of Wales Own Regiment Museum in York for allowing me to use these volumes.

I was very lucky to be able to talk to and record Mrs Doris Adamson, Bill's elder sister, who is a sprightly 92, at her home in Nafferton with the help of her daughter Monica. Her memories about life in Nunburnholme have been used to complement Bill's original text.

I am most grateful to Mr P. Bussey for correcting and commenting on the typed manuscript. Mrs A. Kitching and Mrs M. Brigham very kindly loaned photographs of Warter Priory and gardens. Mr Wilkinson and Mr F. Barker lent me photographs and newspaper cuttings connected with Nunburnholme and Mrs J. Allen, the photograph of Lyndhurst. I would like to thank Mr F.S. Cottom for all his help and encouragement especially with the music and Mr J. Eldon for allowing me to use his recordings of Billy. My parents and wife, Helen, have also been a great help. Mr C. Brook of Hutton Press has been most helpful and I am delighted he agreed to publish this book. Finally, it would have been impossible to continue the project without the support of Bill's daughter, Bridget Harrison, who also loaned many of the photographs.

Peter Halkon,
Cottingham,
March 1989

# Beginnings

I have been asked to write something about my life by two or three people, I hope it will be worth reading. I was born at Nunburnholme on 15th July, 1898 in a cottage in a row of houses called "Black Row". I think it got its name because it had been tarred years before to keep the damp out. When I was a baby I had fits; my parents told me I had thirty in one day and I was laid out for dead twice.

Mrs Wray, who used to help at confinements, put a looking glass in front of my lips to see if there was vapour on it. She would say to my mother,

"Emma, he isn't dead, he's living yet."

Old Dr Fairweather, a Scot, said I was better dead as I would make nothing; I have proved him wrong. Here I am at 86 trying to write something about my life.

My parents were Harry and Emma Harrison. My mother was born at Thorp Arch and her mother lived opposite the Fox Inn. Mother, who was a small, slight woman, came to be the head cook at Nunburnholme Rectory where the Rector, Marmaduke Morris, lived with two sisters, Miss Edith and Miss Laura.

[*Billy's sister relates:*
*"The Morris family used to entertain the Wilsons from Warter Priory in those days. I didn't think the Rev. Morris was very nice. The family were all a bit old fashioned and Miss Edith was the nicest. The other old lady seemed a bit peculiar and none of them were married. Father had two sisters working at the Rectory: one was cook and the other was a housemaid. My father used to bring milk, butter and eggs and such like to the Rectory – that's how he met my mother."*]

Now Miss Edith was the organist, choir mistress and a very good music teacher.

My father was a big man, six feet tall and weighing about fifteen stone. When he got older he used to sup a bottle of whisky a day, but lived while he was 83.

My grandfather Robert was another big fellow who had a beard like a South African Boer. He was broad but lean and as strong as a bullock. My father said he was a lovely bass singer, but I never heard him sing. He died of cancer of the liver at the age of 65. My brother Bob was named after him.

*Bill's grandfather Robert and family in the 1880's. Left to right, back row: Alice, Harry, Jinny, Herbert, Ethel. Front row: Matthew, grandmother, Fred, Lily, grandfather with Rose, Gerty and Arthur. (There may be some inaccuracies here, apart from Harry, Bill's father, due to Doris Adamson's failing eyesight).*

My great-grandfather was called William and that's how I got my name. He had a threshing business and once, so my father told me, he went into Lincolnshire to buy a traction engine and people said: "Old Bill Harrison has gone abroad."

He had only crossed the Humber to New Holland! Later on I drove the same engine.

My father had six sisters, Rose, Gerty, Jinny, Ethel, Lily and Alice. Aunt Rose married a gardener from Warter Priory called Bill Parr. Gerty married Jim Illingworth who worked at the railway carriage works at York; Jinny married a Blacksmith called Jack Spray who lived in Warter for some time and then got a job at the Selby shipyard. Aunt Ethel married an estate agent called Archer who lived in Wales. Lily married a Londesborough farmer, John

Wregghit. Finally Aunt Alice married a parson, Christopher Bourne, who rose to be a canon and they lived at Christchurch.

My father's brothers were Arthur, Matt, Fred and Herbert. Arthur farmed Hessey Farm, Nunburnholme and Matt and Herbert farmed Warrendale farm, Londesborough. Fred was a policeman in Hull and finished up in Market Weighton.

My father's mother came from Starbeck near Harrogate; her maiden name was Simpson.

### Schooldays

*According to Kelly's Directory, the school at Nunburnholme was built in 1855 for fifty-four children and in 1905 had an average attendance of forty-three. It is interesting to note that the departure of Mr Stainer the schoolmaster, appeared to have had an effect on attendance, as this had fallen to twenty-nine by 1913 when Miss Stribbling ran the school.*

I went to Nunburnholme school before I was five years old where we had a very good school teacher called John Stainer. He lodged at Hessey Farm and eventually married Grace Tindale who was a maid at the Rectory. Nunburnholme was very lucky to have a teacher like him; he turned out some very good pupils. Mr Stainer taught music at the school as well as other subjects, so I got tuition free. I used to be asked to come to the front of the class to sing scales to the accompaniment of the harmonium.

Mrs Wilkinson who was called Miss Bree before she was married, used to come every Monday and Wednesday afternoon to teach the girls sewing.

*[Doris remembered more about the school:*
*"There was just one big class-room in the school, with long desks, side by side which was heated by an old black, coke stove. I remember getting pushed off the school steps by Minnie Brigham, who didn't like me. I went clean head first.*
*"You bugger!", I swore.*
*The vicar got to know about this and as I was a choir girl he said:*
*"Doris, it can't be you talking like that!"*
*It was Vicar's day at the school and he found me standing in a corner. Mr Stainer caned me for that. I was ashamed, you know, it*

11

*Nunburnholme School c. 1905. Bill is second from the right on the back row and Doris is fourth from the right in the second to back row. The schoolmaster, John Stainer, can also be seen with Mrs. Wilkinson.*

*Nunburnholme Church.*

*The village school treat at Nunburnholme Rectory in the early 1900's. Mr. Stainer can be seen on the extreme left. The rest of the group is made up of the village choir and the staff of the Rectory. The Reverend Marmaduke Morris stands to the right of the picture, wearing a black hat.*

*came out so pat, but I might have hurt myself on the steps.*

*There was a pupil-teacher at the school called Annie Brigham and the lads dared brother Bob to give her a kiss, which he did – and got caned for it."*

I liked the school and got to number seven class, which was quite good in those days.

I can't tell you how old I was when Mr Stainer left to take a new appointment at Garton on the Wolds, which was a bigger school. A woman teacher called Miss Stribbling, who was fairly tall and strict, followed him.

*[Doris mentioned that,*

*"One teacher (not Miss Stribbling) died; she committed suicide. She*

*was lodging next to Hessey Farm and had got a bit friendly with a man in the village. She got into trouble and one evening, mother saw her go past our window towards the school. She was found hanging in the school porch. Mother often used to say that she wished that she hadn't been near the window. It was a great pity as the teacher was a nice woman."]*

I certainly liked Mr Stainer best. In later years I used to visit him at Garton, cycling there on Sunday afternoons to have tea with him and his wife. He played the organ at the church and I used to sing in the choir.

Now I was a good singer and had joined the Nunburnholme church choir at the age of five and that is where I learned most of my music.

When you went to Nunburnholme church you had to be quiet. One time I turned my head and the school master who was sitting in the pew behind knuckled me on the back of the head. If I had my time again I wouldn't be an Anglican, I would have joined the Salvation Army or Methodists as their services were livelier.

*In his "Yorkshire Reminiscences", the Reverend Marmaduke Morris writes about the choir which he formed, giving a somewhat different perspective from that given by Bill.*

*"We soon got together a few men and children to form a choir and first my mother and then my sisters took them in hand...they were a very tractable and teachable lot and unlike most village choirs never had any wranglings or disputings...With patience and careful training they soon improved. At length when the choral competitions at York were inaugurated our Nunburnholme choir entered for them and they repeatedly gained first prize and were always highly commended even though they were the smallest choir of all....There are few things more delightful in vocal music than a really well trained country church choir."*

## Holidays at Londesborough

When I was at school, we used to get a six week holiday at Harvest and as soon as we left school at four, I got my tea and my mother used to pack my best clothes in a bag and I set off to walk to my grandfather's at Londesborough, which was about two miles away.

The Harrison family had farmed at Warrendale Farm, Londesborough for years, perhaps seventy. All the Londesborough farms were owned by Lord Londesborough.

Grandfather owned a threshing set which comprised a steam engine and a threshing machine and he went from farm to farm threshing the farmers' corn stacks.

I have done the same job. He used to get up at three in the morning, get steam up and be ready to start threshing by seven. It was a dirty job in the winter.

We used to get up at half-past five in the morning. My first job was to fetch the cows from a field called 'The Avenue', going towards Shiptonthorpe. I used to give them a feed, milk one and leave the rest to the 'Bullocky', as we called the cowman. When they had been milked it was time for breakfast. Although I had to work, I didn't mind as we lived well. We had home fed bacon for breakfast followed by fruit pies. There was a plum tree near the farm that produced yellow plums called harvest plums. My grandmother, being an expert cook, knew how to make pies; her apple and custard pies were out of this world.

Now I would like to mention Sunday dinner. The beef wasn't cooked right through and the blood used to follow the knife. There was what we called a well; as you carved the joint, blood used to drop into the well on the meat dish. A tablespoon of this mixed with the gravy, on your Yorkshire pudding and vegetables, followed by a milk pudding or an apple pie and custard and you could do some work!

After breakfast I used to fetch 'oven wood', as we called it, to shove under the oven to get it hot for roasting and baking. I used to chop sticks for lighting the fire in the morning. Before doing these chores I took the cattle back to the field. When I got back to the farm the men would be in the harvest field ready to go, but that depended on the weather. Before a binder could operate, the field has to be 'opened out' as it was called. The men had to go, one with a scythe and one with a nine-tine rake, to make an opening big enough for the binder to operate. The man with the rake used to gather plenty to make a sheaf and then he had to make a straw band to tie it up. There used to be many thistle so it wasn't a good job. In later years I have used both the scythe and the rake. When the binder had cut six rows of sheaves two men would start stooking. Now if I was walking about in the field one of the men would shout.

'Thoo might as weal be doin summat, so throw us outside sheeavs.'

I think it took six rows of sheaves to make a line of stooks. This was supposed to be my six week holiday, of course, but I didn't mind. It was surprising how much I learned in those six weeks. If it was a wet day, the men would mend corn bags with what they called a 'poke needle'. That was a curved needle with a big eye so you could thread binder twine through, or 'Massey Harris' as we called it. Other jobs included mucking out horse boxes or cleaning fold yards out. It all had to be done by hand. If there was any rye-straw in the fold yard you had to use a hay knife to cut it. Another job you would get in damp weather was whitewashing the dairy out and sometimes the back kitchen; there was always a job to be done on the farm whether it was fine or wet.

They used to make butter in those days on the farm using a churn. There were two kinds of churns, horizontal and end-over-end. My grandmother used to take butter, eggs and cream to Market Weighton every Wednesday in a float, that was a low trap or cart. My grandmother was highly respected by the people of Londesborough. If a person in the village got into trouble my grandmother and the vicar had to sort it out. When I met my grandmother on the street I used to raise my hat to her and the girls used to curtsy.

[*Doris also used to go to visit her grandparents and gives this addition to Bill's account:*

*"I had to behave myself when I went to my grandparents at Londesborough. You couldn't go into a room without knocking. Grandmother used to say,*

*"Did you knock, Doris?"*

*"Yes," I said.*

*"Well I didn't hear you."*

*There's no wonder, because I didn't knock. Grandma used to sit with her back to the door; she used to like a drink on the quiet!"*]

The Rector at Londesborough was called Mr Wilton. He had a daughter who was a very good soprano. There was a tale about the vicar: he was seeing off his wife at Londesborough station, when he gave the tip to his wife and kissed the porter!

Being in the choir at Nunburnholme, I was asked to be in the church choir at Londesborough. Now at Nunburnholme church we

16

didn't wear a surplice. When I first put one on at Londesborough church, how proud I was; I thought I was in Heaven! Uncle Herbert sang bass in the choir and Aunt Lily sang in the choir as well. She had a voice like a lad, it was beautiful to hear her sing. The organist at the church was John Metcalfe from Market Weighton who used to cycle every Sunday to Londesborough to play the organ. He was a wonderful player; I think he was a music teacher at Pocklington school.

I don't think my grandfather had much illness until the last six months of his life. One day when I was with him in the harvest field at Londesborough, he wanted to pass water, but he couldn't. I can picture him now in mind. He said to me,

'Lad, I can't pittle.'

After that day he lived about five months and died of cancer.

# Growing up in Nunburnholme before the First World War

*The Reverend Marmaduke Morris in his book "Nunburnholme – its History and Antiquities", describes the village as it was when Bill was a lad and apart from a few new houses and the demolition and alteration of others, it remains much the same as it was in this description written in 1907.*

*"In shape our parish is somewhat long and narrow, being about three miles east to west with an average breadth from north to south of about a mile and a half. The township lies at the point where the now fertile plain of York meets the western edge of the Wolds...*

*Between the hills in a northerly direction runs a well wooded valley for more than a mile to the boundary of the parish. This pleasing bit of country forms a striking contrast to the woodless wolds in the distance. The valley is watered by a small stream or beck with runs through the entire length of the parish... a belt of wood skirts the lower part of the north wold. The ground here is very steep, hence the name "Bratt" which is given to the wood which grows oak, beech and sycamore."*

*Bill remembers that this slope was so steep that they had to rope the traction engine and threshing tackle to get it up.*

*The village name according to A.H. Smith in his "Place names of the East Riding of Yorkshire", comes from the Old Norse "Brunnum" – at the streams. The prefix "Nun" comes from the Benedictine Nunnery founded in 1150, of which nothing remains apart from low earthworks.*

*Nunburnholme is still dominated by St James Church, which is mainly Norman, but restored as a memorial to the Reverend Francis Orpen Morris, author of many books, the most famous being "British Birds". The church contains a striking decorated Norman arch and the finest Anglo-Scandinavian cross shaft in East Yorkshire.*

*From the top of Totterdown Hill, the original long narrow crofts can be seen behind the houses and cottages. The soil is loam and clay with a chalk gravel subsoil and the acreage of the farmland is about 1,857 acres. The chief crops grown during Bill's youth were wheat, barley, beans, oats and turnips. The principal landowners were the Earl of Londesborough, who was lord of the manor and Lord and Lady Nunburnholme of Warter Priory.*

*The population of the village in 1901 according to Kelly's Directory was 220, although this dropped to 190 by 1921.*

*Only one single storey chalk cottage once so typical of this part of East Yorkshire survives intact. The row of houses in which Bill was*

18

*born was situated near the village green through which Nunburnholme Beck flows. These cottages were demolished in the 1920s.*

*Many of the old village families that Bill describes below, still remain though, and Marmaduke Morris states that the Adamsons, Wilkinsons, Brighams and Harrisons settled in the village in the late eighteenth century.*

When I was born in Nunburnholme, there were three families of Brighams, three of Harrisons, two of Frears, two of Wilkinsons, the Keelings, the Tylers, the Richardsons, the Suggets, the Dressers and the Adamsons. William Frankish, Jack Bell, Mrs Martha Jobson, Alfred Ankers and family, Alf Johnson and family also lived there.

John Brigham lived at Totterdown Farm which he farmed for many years. After he retired his son Bill took over. The Brighams were a large and fine family; seven girls and six boys. Totterdown Farm is about a mile from the village on the left hand side of the hill going towards Londesborough. The hill was called Ward Hill and was almost as dangerous as Garrowby Hill. I have ridden down both on a bicycle and motor bike.

*George Frear and his wife and their son, Harrison and their daughter Sally-Anne. They lived in this cottage, formerly "The Devonshire Arms", Nunburnholme's pub, which was closed by Lady Nunburnholme. Raincliffe House stands on the site of the pub.*

19

*Nunburnholme School (right) with the school cottages (centre). Lily Adamson lived at one half of the school cottages and John Dresser, the cartman at Water Priory, in the other.*

William Wilkinson farmed at Manor Farm for a number of years; his son Frank took it over after he retired. Frank had two brothers and a sister, George, Charlie and Janet. George was a joiner, Charlie was a postman and Janet stayed at home until she was married to Eric Maddison. Their son Freddie joined the police force.

George Frear lived in a thatched house opposite the beck. In later years it was pulled down and a new one built, called Raincliffe House. George and his wife had two children, Sally and Harrison. George was a joiner by trade but took to farming. It was a small farm with a few cows, pigs and poultry . He also had a wagonette which would hold about seven people. He used to take them to Pocklington every Saturday for a fare of a shilling return. Harrison Frear used to drive it. His sister Sally was a big friend of my mother. They used to bring parcels for people. My mother used to get a book called 'Home Chat', for which Sally charged a ha'penny carriage. After my mother had finished reading it, Sally got it for nothing! Harrison used to put up at the 'Oddfellow's Arms' at Pocklington. The pub had a travellers' room (called the Market Room) for them and their parcels.

George Frear's brother Tom lived near the chapel. He also had a bit of land. I don't know how he managed to make a living, but he managed to bring up a family. They didn't drink or smoke and never went out anywhere, but that was what life was like in those days. When I was a boy, farm butter was about 10d a pound, and you could buy a packet of Woodbine cigarettes, five for a penny. Tobacco was $3\frac{1}{2}$d an ounce and matches were 1d a box. Eggs cost 8d per dozen and a sheep's head a shilling.

Alf Johnson was a bricklayer on the Warter Estate. He was married and had one son called Billie. Jack Bell was his mate or labourer. They used to argue a lot. One day when they were working at the Priory, I heard Jack say to Alf,

"Ha can knock a nail into a bit of wood as good as thoo!"

"Thoo can't Jack, thoo sees I'm a tradesman and thoo isn't," replied Alf.

Jack Harrison (no relation) was the Roadman. His work was to keep the village tidy. He kept a cow and had pigs and poultry. Now there was George Bones, who also kept a cow and I remember when my mother was baking, she would say to me,

"Slip doon to George Bones and fetch me a jug of ord milk."

It cost a penny. He also sold cream which cost about 3d a cup. I would be sent to fetch it for Sunday tea.

There was a village shop; Matthew Swallow had it and his son Dan took it over after he died. His wife Emma used to bake bread and sell it to people in village. We used to go down on a winter's night to play dominoes, buy a bottle of pop and talk about the events of the day. They liked us to go down as we were company for them. Jack, Dan's brother, used to live with them. One night he was sitting by the fire and said to his brother,

"Dan, can thoo smell owt?"

"Naa", Dan said "thoo's allus smelling summat."

"Summat stinks", said Jack, who was sitting near the airing cupboard.

Now Mrs Swallow had a fluffy white cat, it had got into the cupboard somehow. When Jack opened the cupboard door the cat jumped out. Dan got hold of a walking stick and chased the cat round the house. He was hitting everything but the cat and shouting,

"I'll kill the mucky sod!"

You see the cat had shitten in the cupboard. Next time I went into the shop I noticed that he had the armchair tied with a band which

*Nunburnholme Post Office and shop. Dan and Emma Swallow who ran it can be seen on the right, with Bill's sister Doris and Charlie Wilkinson with cycles. This picture was taken during the First World War, when Doris described her postal round. The gable end fell down in the 1920's.*

was fastened to the cupboard door.

Every New Year, Mrs Swallow used to make frumerty out of creed wheat and a noggin of rum. She used to put black treacle in as well. Anybody who called could have some, that was the custom in those days.

[*According to Doris:*

*"Mrs Swallow used to make a cheap Christmas cake and at Christmas, everyone who came into the shop was offered something. There was no "Public" in the village so people enjoyed visiting them. If they wanted a drink, they would have to walk all the way to the "Plough" at Hayton.*]

Bob Brigham was a tall thin man who had a son called Harold and a daughter called Dorrie. Harold was a good singer, especially when he had had a pint or two at the Pub at Hayton. People used to ask him to sing and his favourite song was 'Freddie Archer'. I have never heard anybody sing that song since. Now his sister Dorrie had a very good contralto voice and used to sing in a quartet. In the winter months, Both worked for my father feeding the threshing machine and when I was old enough I used to cut the band round the sheaves and hand them to him.

He was also the "Flaggy", carrying the flag in front of the threshing machine when it was on the road. Feeding sheaves into a threshing machine was a skilled job. If there was any corn left on the straw, the farmer used to grumble like hell.

Tom Brigham worked at Warter Priory gardens, He had four children, Gerty, Hetty, Winnie and David. Gertie was a housekeeper for a farmer and Hetty married Percy Moor, a local farmer whose corn we used to thresh. Their father Tom, lived to be ninety. He was ill in bed when Jack Harrison went to see him. Jack went home after seeing him and told his daughter that he didn't want to be like old Tom Brigham.

Another Nunburnholme character was William Frankish, who wore two gold earings. It was said in those days that they improved your eyesight. The Durrant family were also active in the village; Jim and Albert were bellringers in the church and along with their brother Herbert played in the village cricket team. The Chandlers had two sons, Joe and Sid, who went to school at the same time as me. We used to fight sometimes. Their father Bill, who worked at Nunburnholme Wold, had a fixed-wheel bike with one brake and two bars on the front forks to rest his feet on. One day he was riding down the hill from work when he lost his footing on the pedals. He put his foot on the bars and trusted to luck. The brake failed and how he stayed on that bike, I don't know! He went through Nunburnholme beck and grazed the wall of George Frear's house. Neither he nor the bike was any worse for wear. When I asked him what it was like going down the hill at that speed, he said it was a bit scarey. In later years he emigrated to Canada, where he did very well.

Arn Johnson and his wife Polly lived in a small cottage near the beck. Mr Johnson, who was a big, gruff sort of chap, worked at Nunburnholme Wold. Us lads used to get a day or two off school to go to pull ketlocks or brassacks out of the corn and Mr Johnson was in charge of us. We were paid a shilling a day; we liked the job as it was a change from school. Mrs Johnson used to be cook for Eldred Young of Londesborough before she was married. The Johnsons kept a cat, tied up like a dog during the day and at night it was let loose. There was many a rabbit on the doorstep of their house next morning. The cat didn't seem to mind being tied up.

At that time there was a row of whitewashed cottages called White Row. A family called the Puckerings lived in the first of these. Now Mr Puckering fell ill and the doctor was sent for. When he came, he told Mrs Puckering to give her husband some chicken broth. This broth didn't do much good as the man died before the doctor left the village!

I never liked funerals: when I was a lad I remember that everybody was dressed in black, and it cost people ever so much to buy black clothes.

Another family of Johnsons lived in the middle of White Row for some time before they moved to Yapham. They had a daughter who married Jim Frear and they moved into the middle cottage when the others went to Yapham. Jim used to play cricket for Meltonby and was what we called a 'square hand' bowler. He was left handed and used to bowl round the wicket and was a bit tricky to play. I remember that he used to play in a Bowler hat.

In the end cottage there lived a family called the Tylers; Billy, his wife, sons George and Fred, and daughter Jinny. George was in the choir and was a good singer. When he got older, he went to live in the West Riding. Now Fred died from lockjaw. He was playing with stack pegs and stuck the point in the middle of his hand, which killed him. While I was still a schoolboy, my grandfather demolished the old cottage where I was born in Black Row and built a new house for my father, called "Wold View".

[*According to Doris:*

*"Mother used to say he was a silly man for building it right onto the pavement when there was a large plot of land available, but my grandfather wanted to build it on the foundations of "Black Row". There was a greenhouse at the end where my father used to sit and talk with his friends. He used to take his fiddle in as well."*]

The new house had a living room, front room, dairy, back kitchen with a copper where we used to wash and three good sized bedrooms. There was also a coal house, a tool house with a hand drill, vice, stocks and dyes. The lavatory was an earth closet; there was no water laid on in those days and everyone had water tubs. These got filled when it rained, from the roof of the house.

*The village green and Nunburnholme Beck, c.1912. Arn Johnson and family lived in the white house, Keelings, Bells and Frankishes in the other cottages.*

*Wold View, built by Billy's grandfather on the site of Black Row cottages. Bill's father Harry is standing on the pavement in a white smock. Hessey Farm is on the right.*

Another memory from my childhood are the visits of the "Wold Rangers". I have been reading a book about them. These were the people who lived rough as their choice of living. Some of these were pleasant, others were not. I didn't know any of these people who are written about in the book, but I knew three that used to travel through Nunburnholme and Warter. One was called Long Harry and he mainly made his home at Warter. I think he slept on a farm in the village. He worked for the farmers, doing odd jobs. He also used to follow Bramby's threshing set, and when the Estate had a shooting day, he went bush beating. He was a tall boney man and the tale was in those days that he would wash his shirt in the pond at Warter, wring it out and put it on again. He was a tough man. Now these people had a code amongst themselves and used to tell each other where there was work; if one could not get a job, they passed it on. One of these men was called Pudding Jack. If I remember rightly he was short and ragged. I have been told that he was given his name because he liked Yorkshire Pudding. I don't know much about him, only that he was friendly and was well liked wherever he went.

Another of these men was called Soldier Tom. He was a big man with a white moustache. He was friendly and was never turned away when he called at the house to get his can filled with tea. Some of these men used to carry a can and some tea with them and would ask for boiling water. Soldier Tom used to call at our house, and my mother never turned him away empty handed; she would fill his can with water and make him a beef sandwich or give him a piece of pie. Some of these men joined up in the Great War. Most were used to horses and joined the Waggoners' Reserve. They were used for transport, taking shells up to the front. These men were forgotten about. The British Army didn't know how lucky they were having them, all used to handling horses. Sir Mark Sykes knew what he was doing when he formed the Waggoners' Reserve. After the war most of these Wold Rangers returned to their old ways of living rough — it was their life.

# Work at Warter Priory

*The "handsome mansion" of Warter Priory, as it was described in Bulmer's directory for 1892, took its name from the Augustinian foundation which once stood near the site of the present church in Warter village. Nothing remains of the old priory but humps and hollows for it was dissolved during the Reformation. Its successor lay about a mile south west of Warter village surrounded by 300 acres of parkland; its carriage drive which begins on the village green at Nunburnholme, now leads to modern farm buildings as the stately home, which boasted some of the foremost gardens in Britain, was demolished in 1972 and the rubble shoved into the lake.*

*When Bill Harrison was born, Warter Priory was at a peak as its owner, Charles Henry Wilson, Hull Liberal MP and shipping magnate and later Baron Nunburnholme, spent around £1m enlarging and beautifying the house. His wife, Florence Jane Helen Wellesley was the great niece of the Duke of Wellington and was by all accounts almost as formidable as the "Iron Duke". Billy remembered that if she saw a single weed growing on the garden path, somebody would be in trouble. Once when a gardener reported for work with a patch on his breeches he was dismissed by Lady Nunburnholme who said,*

*"I don't allow men to work in clothes like that."*

*Bill also recounted that when the noble couple argued on one occasion, Lord Nunburnholme was overheard to say,*

*"You may have the blood dear, but I have the money."*

*The house itself is described in Bulmer's Directory as being:*

*"...of bricks with stone dressings."*

*Pevsner writes that,*

*"...its general character was Victorian...vaguely Italianate with some Frenchy motifs."*

*The gardens and greenhouses surrounding the house covered over 20 acres. The greenhouses included a peach house, two span vineries, two early vineries, a rock fernery, a palm house, a rose house, two early peach houses, two fig houses, five orchid houses and a gardenia house. The gardens themselves were laced by many winding paths and were noted for three magnificent yew trees, exquisite example of topiary work, lily ponds and many examples of classical statuary.*

*A reporter from the Hull Times (3.9.1927) also writes about the gardens in glowing terms:*

*"The splendour of the flowers, the exotic scents, the laying out of the*

*Warter Priory c.1905.*

*gardens, the terraces, the herbaceous borders all combine to make the grounds a never failing cause of delight...as one passes first one glorious patch then another, one sees lavendar, heliotrope, mignonette, honeysuckle geranium... all perfuming the air with their fragrance. In the beautiful Italian garden, every terrace or path has a characteristic appearance of its own, the shape, the adornment, stone or otherwise, the flowers all combine to make a complete scheme."*

*All this was of course only achieved by the efforts of forty outdoor staff, including the gardeners, one of whom was Bill.*

I left school a week before I was fourteen to work at Warter Priory gardens. The estate was owned by Lord and Lady Nunburnholme. I had to be there at halfpast six. The men started at six. I had to pack my breakfast and dinner out of a shilling a day wage. That was six bob a week and we had to wait a fortnight for it. Men had sixteen bob a week. On Saturday we finished at five. We were the outside gardeners. The inside gardeners lived in a bothy. There were about ten of them, and they looked after the greenhouses where they grew grapes, melons, figs, tomatoes, cucumbers and flowers of different varieties. Orchids were one of the special plants; in fact Warter Priory gardens were some of the

*Lord Nunburnholme*

*Lady Nunburnholme*

biggest in the country. Mr Jordan the Head gardener was an important fruit grower.

My first job working there was paring turves. John Dresser, the cartman, used to go out into the fields and cut grass sods, bring them into an open shed and I had to cut the grass off them. These turves would be about fourteen inches square and I had a kitchen knife to cut the grass roots out. After an hour and a half of doing this, I had blisters on my hands. It wasn't a very good job but you had to start at the bottom.

Now Henry Wilkinson was the Head gardener's lad. Henry got promoted, so I got the job. Mr Jordan had a wife and four or five daughters. I had their shoes to clean every morning. Mr Jordan used to wear britches and leggings in winter, so I was kept busy. I used to

*The Saloon, Warter Priory.*

*Warter Priory at the turn of the century with the lake into which the demolished remains of the house were shoved in 1972.*

*Two fashionable ladies enjoy the "Italian" Gardens at Warter Priory.*

get a cup of tea and a piece of cake every morning, so it was better than paring turves.

That job didn't last very long and the foreman gardener, Sidney Legge, wanted me down in the garden. Mr Legge was very strict and you didn't argue with him. Warter Priory was one of the best places to learn gardening, so I will tell you about the gardens. There were the Pleasure Gardens around the Priory itself, and about a quarter of a mile away was the Greenhouse. Adjoining the Greenhouse were the Kitchen gardens. Some of the gardeners there were Robert Smith from Warter, and William Frankish and Tom Yates who lived at Nunburnholme. Robert Smith and his wife had a shop near the village pond. They nicknamed Mrs Smith 'Nellie Bobs'. Two joiners, Alf Ankers and Tom Flint, worked at the gardens making wheelbarrows, seed boxes and painting, repairing and glazing the greenhouses.

Tom used to cycle from Pocklington every morning on a bike with a back-pedal brake. Alf lived in Nunburnholme and used to cycle to work. As I was sitting by the fireside writing this book, I thought of another man who used to work at the gardens, called George Train, who walked from Pocklington every morning, a walk

*The funeral of Lord Nunburnholme, at Warter 31.10.1907.*

of about three and a half miles. He would have to leave home at five, getting to work at six. Some people call them 'the Good Old Days'; how would that man feel when he got home at night after working for ten and a half hours? Times wanted to change; the working man was down-trodden. If you complained about anything, you got the sack and had to go on Parish Relief. Today you get dole and redundancy money. I have lived in both bad and good times and I know which are the better days.

Lady Nunburnholme used to drive round the estate and stop at the workers' cottages. Without knocking, she would throw open the door and inspect to see if everything was in order.

[*According to Doris,*
*"She even used to look in the ovens to make sure there wasn't a pheasant roasting that had been taken from the estate."*]

One woman got so cross that she shouted out to Lady Nunburnholme's groom,

"You can tell her ladyship to put the cottage where the monkey puts its nuts!"

The groom had to tell her.

*Mrs. "Nellie Bob" Smith outside her shop in Warter.*

Lady Nunburnholme always looked after her own herbaceous border. Her favourite flowers were hollyhocks and delphiniums. I used to pick up the rubbish and weeds which her ladyship threw on the path. I still have a little garden trowel once used by her.

I got to know many people on the estate. These are the ones I knew best. There was Ben England, the head keeper, Bob Wilkinson, the estate bricklayer and Sam Hudson, the joiner. The head butler was called Mr Rodgers and the electrician, John Tasker was in charge of the engine that supplied the house with electricity. In those days, when someone retired from working at the big house his son would take over his job and some sons got other jobs on the estate. The son of Mr Matthews, became chauffer to Lady Nunburnhoime. Ben England, a tall man with a short beard, who scared me a bit as a lad, had a son called Tom who took over from him. Tom was a stoutish chap whom I liked very much. Mr Rodgers, the head butler was a big man and certainly made for the job. He was always smartly turned out and very correct in his manner. John Patrick, who was a very pleasant, quiet man, had three sons who all worked on the estate. Jim worked in the gardens at the same time as me and was a very good friend. Ephraim worked in the greenhouses and did very well in the gardening world, being

34

*The pleasure gardens, Warter Priory.*

*The "Italian" gardens, Warter Priory.*

*The scale of the gardens can only be appreciated in this aerial view, taken in the 1950's. It has changed little from the time of Lord Nunburnholme.*

very good at growing carnations. He became Superintendent of Parks in York and then went to Southport. If my memory serves me right, he had his first week in the gardens with me showing him the routine. Now Ephraim hadn't been working long when I was instructed by Mark Moor, the foreman, to weed a miscellaneous border in the graveyard. Lord Nunburnholme and his son were buried there. I said to him,

"If thoo hears a grunt and a moan it will be his Lordship turning over in his coffin, he gets very stiff ligging in ya spot."

The lad said, "I aren't stopping doon here on me own!" I had to stay with him while we finished weeding the border!

John Dresser, the cartman when I started working at the gardens, was a podgy sort of chap who lived in Nunburnholme. He sang in the church choir and had an allotment comprising a garden, sheds, grass and a few hens which used to roost in the cow shed. One morning he was counting them before going to work when one of them dropped a blob in his eye. Well he swore, jumped about, got his hay fork and slayed the lot. He wasn't a really bad fellow though. John Dresser had a few fruit trees at the end of his garden. One of these trees produced really sweet apples and us lads used to go and pinch some. We made sure we knew where he was before we pinched any. One day he thought of an idea to stop us. He dug a cesspool, camouflaged it with leaves and grass expecting to catch us in it. He waited for us, expecting one of us to drop in, but we spotted it. He started to chase us and forgetting about the cesspool, dropped in it himself! You can imagine the language he used.

Once when John Dresser's back was bad, his wife bought a bottle of Sloan's linament. It was a new product that hadn't been out long and she thought she'd try it on his back. Now it said on the bottle that you hadn't to rub it in, but just dab it on the spot where the pain was. Mrs Dresser was doing this when her husband said,

"That's no damn good, rub it in!"

"It says on the bottle just dab," replied his wife.

"To hell with that, just rub it in!"

Well she did as she was asked and John put his shirt back on and started to go to work. He was certainly very pleased to get home as he couldn't bear his shirt on. His wife then had to get some cream to ease the pain. I don't think he ever used Sloan's again.

### Winter Work

I worked at Warter Priory during the summer and used to give my mother half of my wage if she was short of money. In the winter I worked for my father threshing.

My grandfather had set up the business when he brought a threshing set which consisted of a traction engine, a threshing machine and a straw elevator. We had a round which consisted of farms at Hayton, Burnby, Everingham and Nunburnholme and several outlying farms. In those days it was a good living though I used to get nothing apart from my keep and a Sunday suit.

When I worked for my father, I used to get up at half-past four in the morning. If you grumbled they would say;

"We brought you up, we clothed you, what more do you want?"

I don't regret what I did for my parents.

My grandfather's engine was made by Aveling and Porter. Later on I drove other kinds of machine as well such as Fowler, Garret and Burrel. They were all different to drive as some had their steering wheel on the right, others on the left. It was the same with the reverse lever. The engines had a safety plug filled with lead which was fitted in the boiler over the fire-box. If the machine ran out of watter, the lead in the plug used to melt and the steam used to put the fire out. It was a skilled job driving a traction engine. My father's threshing machine was a John Fowler of Leeds. We used to wash the boiler out every now and again. Now when you were threshing on a farm, you would have a water cart or a pump to get the water for the engine, but travelling on the road you had to stop and draw water from ponds or streams. All engines had a suction pipe, which screwed onto a steam cock. The other end of the pipe had a nozzle with holes in it which you dropped into the water. You then turned on the steam cock tap and drew water into the engine. Once we were threshing at Burnby Wold, which was farmed by the Scotts. I had a chap called Tommy Nichols cutting the bands which were tied round the sheaves of corn. He came from York to Nunburnholme, where he lodged with a woman called Lily Adamson in a cottage near the school. It was nearly dinner time when he said,

"Thoo es a great owd rat in tha box."

That's what they called the place where I used to stand to feed the sheaves of corn into the drum. The drum was made of iron and was about three feet six inches long. When you put the sheaves in the drum it beat the ears of corn against a concave, which separated the corn from the straw. When my father stopped the engine, he started taking the clinker out of the fire-box. If you didn't do this, they would block the firebars and stop the draught. I got out of the box and picked up a hay fork and started cleaning the box out. The enormous rat was sitting there, so I stuck the fork into it and threw it over my shoulder. At that very moment my father was bending down clinkering and the rat dropped straight onto his neck as he was bent down clinkering the fire-box. If I'd have aimed I couldn't have been as accurate.

Another time when I was threshing with my Dad at Scott's, the foreman, Tom Oxtoby, went to fetch 'drinkins' for lunch and put the beer down against the waggon shed. When he saw my Dad chasing the dog he shouted, ·

"What's the matter Harry?"

"Didn't thoo see the mucky devil cock his leg up at the bucket and pittle in it?"

Tom said that he hadn't. None of the men would have a drink! My Dad said,

"It's a shame to throw it out, so I'll mull it." After saying this, he put his stoking poker in the fire-box and plunged it into the beer. He did this twice, stirred it and drank most of it himself.

[*Doris relates that:-*

*"Father liked his glass of beer – too much maybe. When he had to move from farm to farm, he went on a bicycle and sometimes I used to fetch him back in the pony and trap. On the main road we had to pass a 'Public', but I said that we weren't going to stop. My father said that we'd just see if the horse stopped. He did, right at the tree where my father used to tie him up outside the 'Plough' at Hayton. I refused to go in for a drink I was so cross."*]

When my grandfather was threshing at Nunburnholme Wold once, it happened to be broth day. Everyone, including the hired men, went in for their dinner. The labourers' wages included this. The foreman was dishing out the broth into basins and one of the men was stirring his and put it to one side. When asked why he said that he had found a dead mouse in it. My grandfather replied,

"I must ha' swalled one, thinking it was an onion stalk."

At some farms the hired men drank their tea out of basins. I knew one chap who went home to collect his washing and said to his mother,

"The buggers must think we are pigs and drink our tea out of bloody basins!"

There was no electric light on farms in those days, and the men used hurricane lamps which they even took with them when they went to bed. When the men had done a day's work, they went in for their tea and after that had to go into the stables and groom and bed up the horses with straw for the night. They would then spend a couple of hours in the saddle house, or 'slum' as they called it before going to bed. It was all bed and work. When my father was hired out once at his uncle's farm, he was paid £5 a year. His uncle also bought him a suit of clothes which cost about 25s.

In those days some farm workers' wives used to work in the farmhouse. They would get free milk and scraps, which were bits of beef or bacon, or bones to make broth. It all helped to swell a family's income. Some of the workers lived in the farmers' cottages which were tied to the farm. At Harvest, farmers hired a man for a month and after that he might get a job thatching the stacks, that meant covering the stacks with wheat or rye straw. You would pull it out of the straw stacks after it had been threshed; to keep the straw straight you used binder twine and stack pegs. Thatching stacks was a skilled job and had to be done to keep water out.

*Bill's grandfather's threshing set outside Hessey Farm, Nunburnholme, 1900. Billy's grandfather is the bearded man on the threshing machine. Bill's father, Harry, is standing on the wheel of the traction engine. Notice the rat by the sign board!*

# The Great War

As time went by, there were rumours of war with Germany, which finally broke out in August 1914. At first, I wasn't fit for service because of an impediment in my speech; I had a terrible stammer and they told me that I would be no good at passing messages down the line. As the war went on, they became short of men. The army sent me my calling up papers in 1917, because conscription had been introduced the year before and it did not matter then whether you stammered or not!

On February 15th, I reported to Beverley Barracks. It was very cold and frosty that morning and there were no fires in the room where we went. There were about forty or fifty of us there, all wearing nothing but our socks and we went in two by two to be examined by two doctors. When it came for our turn, they tested our chests and then we had to bend down. They tapped our private parts with a pencil and told us to cough, looked to see if we had piles and then we got dressed. We all had to report to an office where we were given the King's shilling and signed our names. Now we were soldiers. We got kitted out with second hand uniforms; mine had a bullet hole in the breast which had been sewn up. It had belonged to some poor soldier. I got a pair of size ten boots which were far too big as I took size eight and a half. The storeman said that I would cover more ground! After being passed fit and getting our uniforms issued, we were sent to our rooms in the barracks for the night.

For our first breakfast we had boiled bacon. A barrack room orderly had it in his hands in layers and dished it out like a pack of cards. Mine dropped on the floor and he told me to pick it up and eat it, which I did. That was my first breakfast in the army. We paraded in the barrack square and learned how to form fours and other drill. I met a lad that first day whose name was Alan Foster. His father had a pub in North Cave at that time. We got talking about our homes and parents and what our jobs had been before the war. He said he was a groom. We got along famously and he was a good pal.

That first day the old sweat who was in charge of the barracks offered to show us how to put our puttees on for a tanner. We all gave him the money and it was well worth it. The first Sunday we went for church parade in Beverley Minster. You never saw such a rag-tag lot in your life! We had been at Beverley a week when

*Bill as a new recruit, 1917.*

rumours were flying about that we were about to be moved. One morning after breakfast, we paraded on the square and the commanding officer addressed us:

"You are going to a training camp," he said, "and I want you all to respect your officers and obey orders. The camp you are going to is a good one and I wish you good luck".

We all marched to the station and were entrained. Nobody knew where they were sending us, but I said to my pal that we would know by the stations that we passed through. Anyway it turned out to be in the north at Seaton Sluice, near Newcastle on Tyne. The sea was only a few minutes walk from the camp which was called Astley Arms Camp. We were marched into a field and formed up. In this field there were wooden huts which were all numbered. My pal and two lads from Pocklington called Field and Hunter had the good luck to be in the same hut, number seventy-one. Eventually we got our new uniform, two per man. One was for training and the other for walking out. We were also given a swagger stick for when we went out; if you met an officer, you put the stick under your left arm and saluted with your right. We also got a kit bag, proper size boots as well. It was a good camp and plenty of food was provided. Our officers were all decent fellows, as decent as army life permits, that is. We were all given a number; mine was 52273. Our training consisted of P.T., football, boxing and running. I preferred boxing as I didn't like football. They put me in the left back position in one game and I saw this fellow coming to tackle me, so I said that he could have the ball as I didn't want it. I stuck to boxing.

We were issued with a rifle which had a magazine holding five cartridges and aperture sights. There was a short bayonet to fix on the barrel end. We only trained with these rifles, never using them for firing. I think they called them Lee Metfords. The rifle we used in the war was called a Short Lee Enfield which was an improvement on the one we trained with. The first time we fired it was on a miniature range at the camp. As time went by we moved to Whitley Bay to fire on the big range. Now this was a test to see if we were any good at hitting a target at one hundred yards and further. I passed out a first class shot, just missing marksman by one bull.

Our battalion was a Training Reserve Battalion, and our cap badge was a soldier's button. As time went on, me and my pal Alan Foster were walking in Blythe with two other chaps on a Saturday afternoon, when somebody gave me such a clap on the back. I turned round to see Ronald Thompson, whose father had the Post Office at Burnby, the next village to Nunburnholme. Ron was a postman in civilian life. After having a good chat and laugh we went our way and I didn't see him until after the war when he returned home to take up his duties as a postman again.

[*The Great War affected Nunburnholme like many other Wold villages. Bill's father became a special constable and both Bill and his elder brother joined up; Bill in the 2/6th West Yorkshire Regiment and Bob in the East Riding Yeomanry. Doris became a postwoman at Nunburnholme.*

*"I had to do something, so I got to be post lady. I used to go to Burnby Station to meet the train, get the bag and take it to Burnby Post Office where we had to do the sorting. I was provided with a bicycle and my round included Nunburnholme, part of Warter and then round the hilltops to Londesborough. I used to walk down Totterdown hill because it was so steep. I had to sign on at Burnby and sign off at Nunburnholme but I used to be late sometimes. On one occasion I arrived late and when the postmaster asked where I had been, I said that I had had a head wind. I hadn't at all. There was a little keeper's cottage on Silver Valley near Warter and the people there used to ask me to play a tune for them on the piano. Another farmer often used to shout to me,*

*"It's broth day – come and have some and play for us!"*

*I was late again and I nearly got the sack. At Christmas when I couldn't carry all the parcels on my bicycle, my Dad took me on the round in his pony and trap. I used to have a job to get him away as in every house we called at, people would say,*

*"Harry, we don't often see you round this way, stop and have a drink."*

*Of course we were late again and I hadn't a head wind then.*

*Once at Burnby when I was reading a postcard that someone had sent me, the postmaster shouted,*

*"Hey missus, you shouldn't be reading the mail on your round."*

*Mrs Ankers at Burnby got her letters back – her son Alfred was killed in the trenches. The poor woman used to say,*

*"Oh dear, is there another one."*

*My mother was lucky as both her sons came back."*]

There was a measles epidemic in the camp of which I was a victim so they took me to a hospital in Newcastle. We were there for a fortnight or so, when I was asked to take some lunch to a chap in a room of his own. It turned out to be none other than Ronald Thompson's brother from Burnby! I told him I had just met his brother in Blythe and he just replied that it was a small world.

I got better and returned to camp, where I had to report to the orderly room. I was given a pass for six days leave and a free railway warrant. Going home to see my mother was great and she was proud to see me in uniform.

While I was at Astley Arms Camp I met another person whom I knew from Pocklington, a professional pianist with letters behind his name called Bert Buttle. We both got a shock when we met. He was in charge of concerts and entertainment for the camp.

As we had just about finished our training, there were rumours that we were about to be moved again to another camp. The Army never tells you where you are going; you were told to get your kit and either marched or went by lorry to the next place. We went by train and stopped at Ipswich. We all got out, formed fours and started marching. Eventually we ended up at Blackheath Common, where we slept in bell tents, twelve to each tent. We propped our rifles round the pole of the tent. Everybody got dysentry there because we only had one bowl of water to wash in between the twelve of us! This was more like active service, and I was wishing I was back in Northumberland. What with the dust and shortage of water and the dysentry, they had to move us to another camp. This camp was called Lattice Barn Camp and was in the town of Ipswich. Conditions here were much better.

Half of the battalion were going to Felixstowe for a fortnight's training, which consisted of signals, Lewis gun training and more rifle training with a new weapon they called the Japanese rifle. I went with the second half; when the first half went we paraded and I happened to be on the front rank. When the officer in command of the parade called for a volunteer to look after the catering, nobody responded. As he was walking about he suddenly stopped in front of me and said,

"You look like a likely lad for the job. Report to the cooks."

The officer's name was Lieutenant Butters. It was a big job to undertake, but the cooks showed me how to do it and I managed alright. The food we got here was different to that we got in Northumberland; it was soldier's rations. In Northumberland, at Astley Arms Camp, we would sit about sixteen to a table, with an

N.C.O. in charge. We had two plates per man, one for porridge and the other for tripe, bacon and egg or liver for breakfast, stew or meat pie with a crust of Indian cornflour for dinner and two slices of bead and jam or marmalade for tea.

The time came for us to return to Ipswich. We got down to our usual training, which consisted of route marches, P.T., assault course, how to handle a Mills bomb and the 'stick' bomb. This bomb was placed down the barrel of a rifle, which was strengthened to take the special cartridge which sent the bomb fifty to a hundred yards. It was a very useful bomb for firing at a machine gun post. We also had to go over the assault course wearing gas masks, with fixed bayonets on our rifles. There were special trenches built to practice trench warfare. This consisted of some of the chaps holding the trench and the remainder charging like hell. The men in the trench used to duck when the attackers arrived because they used to jump over the trench and stick a dummy that was supposed to be a German soldier. We found it was different when we got into action in France.

There were more rumours about a move. We had an idea where we were going because we had just about finished our training; we were going overseas on active service. We were drafted to a regiment, the 2/6th West Yorkshire Regiment. When the time came for us to leave Ipswich, we formed up and the C.O. lectured us on discipline. The officers and N.C.O.s who trained us didn't go abroad with us and we got different officers. We had trained from February to October. Before I was called up, the Government were sending men to fight with very little training. We were marched to the station where we entrained. We knew we were going south because of the names of the stations we were going through. I remember saying to my pal Alan Foster that we would soon know if all our training had been any good. Eventually the train pulled up at Dover station where we got out, formed up and marched to the quayside.

### In the trenches at Cambrai

*The 2/6th battalion of the West Yorkshire regiment which Bill joined had been in the thick of the fighting at Bullecourt in April 1917. The next major action they faced was the famous Cambrai offensive of November 1917. The aim of this attack was to break the German front* line, or Hindenburg line as it was called and then gain Cambrai itself. As the ground here was more suitable for mechanised warfare than the Somme had been, the British High Command decided to attempt a new form of attack, using tanks to break through the enemy lines, closely supported by infantry. There was to be no heavy barrage as there had been at the Somme in 1916 as the aim was to catch the Germans unawares.

The 'official' account of the battle and the part played by the West Yorkshire's is given in volume two of Everard Wyrall's, "The West Yorkshire Regiment in the War 1914-1918" Bodley Head 1927) and "The history of the 2/6th Battalion West Yorkshire Regiment" by E.C. Gregory. According to these accounts the 2/6th Battalion which formed part of the 62nd Division, had to capture the village of Havrincourt and the German front line and support trenches. Just before 'Zero hour', 6.20 a.m. on November 20th, the German guns opened fire in a fierce barrage and the British feared that the surprise attack had been betrayed. This died out and all became quiet again. According to the Commanding officer of the 62nd Division, Major General W. Braithwaite, the first phase of the advance was a great success, as "Tanks moved forward in advance of the infantry crushing down the enemy's wire...rolling across the German trenches and driving his infantry to the ground." The West Yorkshires had in fact made a record advance for the British on the Western Front of 6,000 yards in a day. In some sectors the troops faced heavy hostile machine gun fire.

This record gain was only to be held for a short time, as the first heavy counter attack took place on 22nd November at 6 a.m. According to the Battalion history it was particularly fierce, supported by rifle and machine gun fire with the enemy advancing on all sides of the 2/6th, almost surrounding it. The situation was critical as the West Yorkshires had fired all their ammunition and were forced to retire. By 9 a.m. they fell back to a sunken road leading from Bapaume to Cambrai near Bourlon Wood. Despite further attempts to regain the ground the British were pushed back still further. According to one company sergeant-major.

"It had been a great victory, but to be candid, ended in a great defeat".

Casualties were heavy in the battalion, amounting to twenty officers and 260 N.C.O.s and other ranks.

Bill's description of the battle fits in well with the outline of events

47

*Bill in the uniform of the West Yorkshire Regiment. This was taken on leave in 1918.*

given in the Regimental histories but it is far more immediate in the horrific detail it supplies. Bill did not see the end of the battle as he became ill, largely due to the appalling weather conditions which are described in the War Diary, eventually being sent home. The physical and mental impact of his experience on the front remained with Bill for some time after the war and his sister Doris related how she and her mother used to have to put chairs around his bed when he suffered attacks of a nervous complaint.

The time came for us to board the transport which would take us to France. I told my pal Alan that it was going to be a bloody rough passage. I was as sick as a dog. I did notice a convoy of destroyers going round us all the time to protect the troop ships. We landed at Calais and marched to a camp at Étaples. There we carried out more training such as testing our gas masks in a gas chamber. One man took off his gas mask; he wasn't going up the line! How he came on, I don't know. We all lived day by day, nobody knew what was in store for them and I thought it was better to chance your luck at the front line than commit suicide.

We went on a sorting out parade one morning, which was the last I saw of my mate Alan, until the end of the war. He was lucky same as I to get home. We didn't stay at this camp long as it was time for us to go up to the front line. If anyone reads this book, I want them to understand that I am only writing what I remember, I never bothered much about names of villages that we passed through; all I was bothered about was getting through this war alive. We were going up to the front as drafts to make up the numbers of the 2/6th West Yorkshires, who were already there. If my memory serves me right, we marched through Béthune, where we stayed the night and eventually arrived at our camp. We stayed at this camp for ten days, doing a few manoeuvres, especially at night with white tapes for a guide, through woods and fields.

The time came for us to go to the front itself and we took our surplus baggage into the stores. While we were doing this, a Ford car, or 'Tin Lizzie', as we used to call them, drove by. I said to myself that I knew the driver of the car. One of the lads overheard me and told me not to be stupid as I wouldn't know anybody out here. The car stopped, so I went up to it and said to the driver,

"I think I know you, you're Herbert Johnson".

"Yes I am", he replied. Then I told him that I was Bill Harrison from Nunburnholme.

"Good God", he exclaimed, "Black Harry Harrison's lad!"

He was taken aback and did not know what to say for a bit. To make it clear, Herbert Johnson was my uncle from Didsbury. In civilian life he was a chauffer. I told him I was going to the front and he gave me forty francs to buy fags and chocolate and wished me the best of luck.

Now we had to carry the following equipment: a leather harness with two pouches, an entrenching tool, a water bottle, a haversack and a bayonet on the left hand side. As I was number three on a Lewis gun, I had extra stuff to carry; a mills bomb in each pouch of my haversack, 'Iron' rations, shaving kit, cigs and chocolate, the Short Lee Enfield .303, a bandolier of ammunition for my rifle and four magazines for the Lewis gun, in what you called a pannier slung over the left shoulder. These magazines were round and held forty-seven rounds of .303 cartridges, in each. All this was what they call 'Battle Order'.

The 2/6th West Yorkshires had just come from holding the line at Bullecourt and came to the camp for a rest, which is where we joined them. This battalion was part of the 62nd Division. We marched to the front line under cover of darkness, I couldn't tell how far, we just kept on till we reached our objective. As we got nearer to the front I heard bursts of machine-gun fire and lights in the sky, the flares from Very pistols. The Germans were always sending these up.

Eventually we got to the trenches and covered each man in the trench. When this was done, it was their turn to go for a rest. Just before the break of day, the Germans trench-mortared our trench as was their custom every morning. An odd one dropped here and there on each side of us, but all we got was the muck from the blast. I had a charmed life. Eventually the firing stopped and all was quiet. Every man then got a ration of rum. It was strong and felt as though it went down to your feet and gave you a bit of false courage. The first man I saw dead was at Bullecourt. He was one of our lot. I found him laid with half his head blown off; I thought to myself that it could be me next.

Word was passed down the line and we got onto the parapet in extended order, about two or three yards apart. I asked a youth next to me to take the entrenching tool out of my pack. We had been told to dig in. I said that there would be plenty of shell holes to shelter in. Tanks were in front of us, monsters going at about four miles per hour. Then our artillery started to open fire, pounding the German lines and giving us cover. As we started to advance by the break of day, the guns lengthened their range. After a while the barrage stopped because we were getting nearer to the German lines. The tanks I passed were stationary. I passed close to one and I didn't see any sign of life from it, but I didn't have time to look inside. My eyes were glued on the enemy trenches. It was getting lighter every minute and I found I was in front of a German machine-gun post. This is where my training came in; I dropped down on my guts and fired at the gunner. He dropped, whether I shot him or somebody else, I don't know. That was my first shot at the front. When I had fired my course at Whitley bay, I had missed being a Marksman by one bull, though I considered myself as good as a Marksman. I kept crawling for a bit, firing and trying to keep my head down. I then stood up and started walking in line with the other chaps. There were bullets flying everywhere, zip-zip-zip and men kept dropping and I wasn't hit. It was amazing how some get killed and others don't; I have often thought that life is a mystery. Fancy walking towards a trench full of enemy troops firing at you, with much more chance of them hitting you than you them.

We took the German trench. Our losses had not been as heavy as on some other fronts such as Ypres or the Somme. The ground was firm and we were not troubled by wire. We took a few prisoners, but one lad about my age, came out first with his hands up, shouting 'Kamerad!'. One of our lads shouted 'Bastard' and shot him. The chances are that if he had come out with the other prisoners he would have been saved. We took up our positions in the captured trench and waited for the next move. We could see Cambrai in the distance, which was as much as I saw of it.

We had to watch for booby traps in the trench that we had just captured; the Germans would leave bread and chocolates with explosives wired to them; touch it and bang!, up you went.

We held the trench a day and a night. There was a whisper passed down the trench that the Germans were going to counter attack, which proved to be true as they charged our position the next morning in massed formation, shoulder to shoulder. Our captain, a nice fellow with a good voice, had been singing an old song, 'Thora', not far from where I was standing. He was shot. Thousands of the enemy came charging towards us. The other two men on the Lewis gun were shot, number one through the head and number two through the throat. I was the only one left, so it was my turn to take over. I fired and fired into the pack of Germans, but they kept on coming and we were getting short of ammunition. I thought to myself that my luck was going to run out when Sergeant-Major "Silkie" Silkstone passed the word down to get out. The Germans were also straffing our trenches in their bi-planes which had machine guns firing through the propeller. We fell back and watched the reserves come up from a sunken road. I think they were a guards regiment and went for the Germans with fixed bayonets, some of them firing Lewis guns from the hip! It was an awful sight to watch, shouting, screaming and slaughter. Mind you, we had done our job in taking the front line trench. There were one hundred and twenty in our company; at the end of the day there were only ten of us left. We went further back and rested in Bourlon wood.

Our rations came up, hard square biscuits, dog biscuits we used to call them; they took some eating. We had a loaf of bread after we got out, a little lump of white bread for ten. The German prisoners were better fed. We used to have rice pudding in these big 'Dixies' which was unsweetened and tasted awful. We were resting and eating our meal when a German spotter plane flew over head and dropped its signal flares. After a very short time we were shelled, not by ordinary shells, but by Whizz-Bangs which were shrapnel shells designed to explode tree-top high and spread to the ground. You didn't hear them coming till they exploded. My luck stayed with me but one of our chaps went crackers and started running around screaming. He had shell-shock and we had to catch him and hold him down, poor lad. Shrapnel was flying everywhere and we had to lie on the ground with our helmets on the back of our heads and chance being hit anywhere else. I am sorry to say everybody didn't have my luck.

The winter in France in 1917 was bloody rough. The men at the base had a decent bed to sleep on but us chaps at the front kipped down where we could whether it was snowing, raining or freezing. I went sick at Bourlon wood with being wet through; my great-coat was so rotten I just tore the bottom off. There were rats as big as cats eating off the bodies of the dead soldiers. The rats were all over the place and at dark they used to walk over your face to see if you were dead. They wouldn't touch you though. I've had them creeping over me. You got so tired that you could sleep anywhere, 'on a clothes line' as the saying was. I was laid there one night when it was freezing and I could hardly get up and had to rub and rub to get the life back in my legs.

I got nephritis from sleeping in such conditions and was taken to a big hospital which had marquees and proper hospital beds. There a doctor, who was American I think, examined me and put me on a special diet.

I didn't realise how ill I was. I was just 19 years old, but looked younger and a man in the next bed to mine said that it was a bugger that lads of my age were sent out to fight and hoped that I would be sent home to Blighty. I didn't know him, but he said that he was a married man with a family at home. He would be about thirty I guess. He said that he never expected to get home. The M.O. came round one morning and when he got to my bed he said,

"Sonny, I have marked you for Blighty."

I thanked him very much but I was a bit scared as they wouldn't have sent me home for nothing.

I was a stretcher case and was carried onto the ship. I remember that the bed I was in was by a porthole and the sun was shining on a calm sea with the water gently lapping on the side of the ship. It was a lovely day early in the New Year of 1918. The crossing to England was very pleasant and on landing we were sent to London.


## Blighty

In the train with me were a mixture of men, Welsh, Scots, Cockneys and other Yorkshiremen. We all said we hoped they would drop us where we wanted, but the army had their own ideas about this! They kept us northerners down in London and sent the southerners up north; I don't know why they did this but they seemed to put you as far from home as possible.

The hospital that I ended up in was at High Barnet in London. It was a three storey building and they carried me up to the top floor on a stretcher, putting me in a bed near the fire-escape. The Christmas decorations were still up and it was a treat being in hospital compared with the front in France. I was still on a light diet of eggs, milk and rice pudding with no meat at all. It was great to have regular baths and have no lice.

Behind the hospital was an anti-aircraft gun, which used to shoot at the Zeppelins as they dropped their bombs on London. Every time it fired it used to make the whole hospital shake. There was one chap in the ward who had shell-shock and every time the gun went off he would shout and tremble and the nurses would have to quieten him.

As time went by I became stronger and was able to get out of bed. The air-raids didn't bother me, but I worried about those who were still bedfast and couldn't help themselves. The hospital was lucky and was never hit. I used to get out of bed when there was a raid, go to the fire escape and watch the search lights. The Zepps looked like big silver cigars.

When I was mobile, I used to help the nurses. As I had been a gardener before the war, I enjoyed looking after the plants. If the day-sister wanted to pop into the town for half an hour, I would see to the lads by walking them to the toilet, fetching them a bedpan or a drink. I used to get up at half-past five in the morning and help the nurses wash the wounded soldiers. Some of the wounds were horrible and I remember one man in particular who had half his calf missing, all raw flesh. I liked helping and soon became chummy with the men on the ward.

I used to go for walks with two of the chaps to New Barnet. Many retired people lived in this residential area; some of them had been shop-keepers and bank clerks. One Sunday afternoon, we were passing a house when an old lady asked us if we would like to come in for a cup of tea. We went in, sat down and started talking about the war and what it had been like being in France. The reason that the old lady was so interested was that she had lost a grandson at the front. She had his photograph in a frame and asked us to look at it. When I took hold of it I got a shock because he was so much like me that it was like looking at my own photograph. He was the same age as me, but maybe a little taller. As we were leaving, the old lady called me back and asked me if I would come and see her on my own. I did this a few times but knew that I would be leaving hospital soon and I didn't look forward to telling her this as she used to shed a tear every time I visited her. I thought it was best to leave Barnet without her knowing. I couldn't take the place of her grandson in any case, and I was hoping to get back to Yorkshire and home. I have often thought since that I should have written to her and explained.

Us three chaps also got friendly with a police sergeant who asked us if we would like to join him and his wife for a bit of supper. His wife played the piano and so every Thursday night we would got to see them. They were a grand couple and we spent very pleasant evenings with them singing round the piano. I was a fair good singer and they used to get me to sing solos such as 'Perfect Day', 'Thora', 'Home Sweet Home' and then we all used to join in the war songs.

The day came for my final examination. The M.O. had already kept me in the hospital a month longer than he should but he asked me a few questions about how I felt and to my surprise said that he would like to keep me on another month, as I have been such a help to the nurses and patients. I was a fool and ought to have said yes, as

*Convalescent camp at Alnwick, 1918. Billy is standing on the back row on the left.*

it might have saved me from going to France for a second time.

I was given ten days sick leave, but arrived at York station on the first night too late to catch a train home. I was hanging around by the waiting-room when a 'Red Cap', or Military policeman approached me and asked if I'd missed my train home. I answered, saying that I would have to kip down in the waiting-room and catch the first train to Nunburnholme in the morning.

"There's no need for that", he said, "I'll take you to a Soldiers' Rest in the town and there you will get a good bed, a bath and a meal all for free".

As we were walking along he asked me how old I was. I answered that I was nineteen and that I had been over the top at Cambrai and I was starting my ten days sick leave. He asked me for my pass and railway warrant and asked me if I had been wounded. I replied that I hadn't, but had got a serious illness. I think he had taken pity on me as I looked younger than nineteen. At last we arrived at the Soldiers' Rest, I thanked him and then we parted; I shall always remember him.

I caught the train early next morning, got off at Nunburnholme Station and walked home where my mother greeted me with tears in her eyes. My father was different and cheerfully said,

"Ess thou shutten all t'Germans then?". People at home had no idea what it was like out in France and what the soldiers went through. Perhaps it was just as well.

The ten days went very quickly and the time came to say goodbye once more. A few more tears and I was on my way to catch the train to York. I had orders to report to the infantry barracks where I stayed for a week.

One morning, whilst on parade, the sergeant gave the command for some of us to fall-out. I remember him calling out my number 52273. We were told to report to the quartermaster's store, where we collected our kit and then marched to the station.

As the train moved on, I knew that we were going north by the names of the stations on the way. Nobody of course knew what our destination was but eventually we arrived at Alnwick in Northumberland. We all got out, formed up and marched in columns of four to a big convalescent camp, where we were billeted in marquees with tarpaulin groundsheets. We slept on army beds made up of two trestles, three boards and a palliasse filled with straw. We had a bolster filled with straw and two blankets as well as our army great-coats to keep us warm.

I stayed at this camp for over two months. One day when I was walking about I spotted a man whom I thought I knew, so I approached him.

"Are you Sergeant Major "Silkie"?" I asked

"That's me," he replied, "but I don't know you."

"I wasn't far from you in the front line trench at Cambrai."

"Good God," he said, "We were lucky to get out of there!"

We had a good chat and went our way.

Influenza hit the camp and I was one of the many that got it, my temperature being a hundred and three for three days. You can see I wasn't feeling very well! They were carrying out many dead and I just lay there, not bothering whether I died or not. They kept coming round with spoonfuls of medicine which tasted like paraffin.

Luck stayed with me and I recovered, was passed fit and came home on seven days sick leave after which I got orders to report to Whitley Bay. The army had taken over Fun City as a base. I stayed there for a week or ten days and met a man who was a market trader in civilian life; I met him again a year or two later.

My next orders were to report to Earsdon where we did a lot of route marches and P.T. You had to wear full kit in all these exercises to test your fitness.

## With the Army of Occupation

*The next part of Bill's story tells how he joined the 1/6th West Yorkshire Regiment in D Coy, 5th platoon. According to the Battalion history, they were severely cut up by a German tank attack in October 1918, just before Bill arrived back in France. They lost ten officers and 200 other ranks. For the rest of the war they were held in reserve and when Armistice came, they were billeted in the village of Evin Malmaison, about five miles north of Douai. From there they joined the Army of Occupation on the march to Germany. According to Bill, he became batman to Lieutenant Horton. Unfortunately I have been unable to trace any further details concerning this officer.*

I was transferred to the First Battalion of the West Yorkshires, in the Sixth Division, who were regulars. From this camp drafts were sent to France and I was a spare man on one of these, in fact I got on a train once when my name and number were called out, "Private Harrison, 52273, fall out." I reported back to camp. The reason why there was a spare man on the draft was in case a man deserted. I was lucky again, for the draft that went out then, got badly cut up at the front line.

The next draft went out a week later and I was on it. It was October 1918 and I had gone out to France for the first time almost exactly a year earlier, but this time the crossing was much calmer than the first. Eventually we landed and went to a big camp to await orders.

Now there were rumours about an armistice going round which everybody hoped would take effect soon, as we were under shell fire all the time, athough we were in reserve. There were some casualties, especially amongst the transport lines behind the camp. We got used to the shells, it was the bullets that frightened us.

The rumours of armistice continued and at last it came on 11th November. I can't remember where we were but we all paraded that morning and at eleven I could hear some bells ringing. When the colonel announced that the war was over we all cheered, but our work was not over. Our next duty was to march to Germany.

"I want you to act like soldiers," the colonel said, "and behave in the manner in which the British are accustomed to behave."

On the march I got pally with a chap called Cox, who was the first mate I had had since I was parted from Alan Foster. Cox was a nice chap, a little more refined than me with a better education and we got on famously. As the march progressed, we got near the Belgian border. Periodically we rested, sometimes for two days at a time depending on whether the place was suitable or not. There were a lot of men to accommodate and of course we had no beds and just kipped down in barns if we were lucky enough, as most of the villages had been under shell fire. Every man had a waterproof ground sheet and we would just lay this down and flop, dead tired.

One rest day, me and my pal Cox were talking about different things, when he told me about an officer coming to join the platoon from the same district as he lived in. Whether they went to the same high school or not I don't know, as I never asked him. My pal said that he might know him and that he would probably ask Cox to be his batman, but he didn't want the job. He asked me if I fancied being an officer's servant. There were a lot of privates who had had a high school education and had the chance to be officers but would not take the responsibility, as they wanted to be with the lads. Cox was one of these. Now this officer joined us at Dinant and the first morning he took over the platoon he spotted Cox. You could see by the way they were talking that they knew each other. As my mate had predicted, he was asked to be the new officer's batman. My mate told him that he didn't think he could do the job, so he passed it on to me. The officer asked me a few questions and I accepted the job.

We got on famously and he was a grand chap. His name was Lieutenant Horton and he was a full Lieutenant with two stars on his shoulder and tunic sleeves. Before he was transferred to our company, he was in action on the Piave in Italy, where he had won the Military Cross, the ribbon of which I had the pleasure of sewing onto his tunic.

Every day's march saw us nearer to occupying part of Germany. It was a hard job on the march and at the end of every day's journey the quartermaster-sergeant used to shout to the officers' servants to fall-out and carry their master's valises to wherever he was billeted. You then had to get him cleaned up for dinner and in the morning ready for the day's march. He was good to work for and used to call me William.

We stayed for two nights and a day at a small town called

Malmedy where we all had a good bath and got properly cleaned up. The officers were billeted in a small hotel and it was quite a change for them to have a decent bed to sleep in. We servants fared very well those two nights and we got beds, but these were on the floor as the hotel was short of bedsteads. I suppose that most of them had been commandeered by the army for hospitals.

While on the march, I got terrible toothache which I remember very well. We were near the frontier and on the next rest day I reported sick. There were a fair few of us waiting for dental treatment and when it came to my turn I went in and sat on a high stool with an N.C.O. in front of me. The dentist asked me whether I wanted a filling or my tooth out. I said that I wanted it out and without further questions he got hold of it with his forceps and with the N.C.O. holding my arms, he yanked it out. By hell, there was blood everywhere, but my toothache was cured! When Lieutenant Horton asked me how I was, I told him that the dentist had pulled the tooth out with a straight draw and no freezing or numbing. I think the army are more humane these days!

While we were on the march the army took our small arms off us which I thought was a daft thing to do. While resting in a village in Belgium, I picked up a postcard in a house where we stayed for the night. On this card was a picture of two boys, I don't know whether they were German or Belgian lads. I have often wondered whether those two boys lived to fight in the Second Great War, or if they'd been killed in the shelling in the first. I shall never know.

We got nearer and nearer to the German border. In my opinion the German Army was never beaten in the fighting but it was the blockade that starved out the German people and caused unrest in the country. Don't get me wrong, the British soldier is a good fighter, if given the stuff to fight with.

We crossed the frontier at last and saw an isolated house on our left. Three German children were larking about; by hell, didn't they run when they saw us. I have often wondered what they were thinking about as they ran into the house.

Our first night in Germany was spent in a village, but don't expect me to remember the name of this or the other villages we passed through as I didn't keep a diary then. Our billet that night was in a cottage up a lonely lane, about two or three hundred yards from the village. That meant that I had to carry the officer's valise, escort him there, get him cleaned up and escort him back to join his brother officers for dinner and then take him back to the cottage. Remember it was December and on the dark nights on my own, coming back from the cottage I felt a little edgy. I had my side-arm with me and my bayonet, remember we were in an enemy country and you had to be ready for anything. The couple who lived in the cottage were in their sixties and were not very pleasant.

When I woke next morning to get my boss ready for the day's march, I found that he had barricaded the door of the parlour where he had been sleeping and was very pleased to see me when I knocked on his door. He said that the old people had been trying to get in during the night. Our transport officer could speak fluent German, so my boss reported them to him.

Every day's march brought us nearer to our goal which was a village called Erp. We finally got there two or three days before Christmas and on Christmas Day, we even ate our dinner out of dixies. Two other chaps and me were billeted at a small farmhouse, Lieutenant Horton at a small store. The farmer was a man of about sixty, over six feet tall, with a straight back and a military bearing. In fact he told us that he had been a sentry at the Kaiser's palace; he looked the part so we were inclined to believe him. We didn't stay long at that billet as the army moved us to the same shop as Lieutenant Horton, where he had a room on his own, while we three lads slept on the floor in bedrooms, a big improvement from being at the farmhouse.

The village of Erp was stretched out and it was a good long way from our billet to the officer's mess. Now Lieutenant Horton went sick with 'flu and had to stay in bed for quite a long time and I had to carry the little food he could eat all the way from the mess. I asked the M.O. if it was possible for my boss to be moved to the officer's mess, which was a big farmhouse. Well this was organised which meant it was easier for me to attend to him, which was my job. He kept on improving and I had the idea of getting some brandy or something, which I thought might do him good. Without the knowledge of the M.O., I asked the farmer's wife if she had any brandy, or the equivalent, so she looked in the cupboard, brought a bottle out and poured some liquor into a glass. She was putting the bottle back, so I gestured that I wanted the whole lot, which she understood in the end. I started to go upstairs with the glass and bottle in my hands and I thought that I better try some before I gave it to my boss, so I emptied the glass down my throat. By hell it was strong. When I walked into by boss's room with the bottle, he reared up in bed and said,

"What the hell have you got there?"

"Something to do you good," I replied. So I poured him half a glass out and told him that I had sampled it first. He asked me where I got it from and I told him that I daren't go to the mess for some, so I had asked the farmer's wife if she had got any brandy or the equivalent. I told him that he would have to pay for it. It was certainly worth it as he soon got better and was able to resume his normal duties. I got him moved back to his billet, so everything was normal again.

As time went by, Lieutenant Horton was promoted to acting adjutant which meant that his duties were at H.Q. which of course meant paperwork, and another officer came to take his place. This new officer came from the Pocklington area and was called Tom Birket. He stopped me one day after lunch and asked if I was Harry Harrison's son from Nunburnholme. The Birkets were big farmers in the Pocklington area and my grandfather had threshed on their land.

While we were in Germany, the band of the West Yorkshires came over from York to play for us. They used to play in the officers' mess and on ceremonial parades, which was very enjoyable. A contest was held in the mess for the best Sam Browne belt. Now my officer, Lieutenant Horton, had a fairly new belt, so he asked me to see what I could do with it. Well I got cracking on this. The Captain, 'Spit' Rendel, as they called him, had an old belt which was darker and easier to polish. I worked hard on Lieutenant Horton's, but when it came to the night of the competition he came second and the captain's belt won, as I had expected. It was all a bit of fun and the captain's servant got fifty marks for his efforts and my boss gave me the same, as every one had said that it was a toss-up between his belt and the captain's.

The couple who owned our billet were middle-aged and had two sons, one who was a captain in the German army and a prisoner of war in England and the other who was a clerk in a bank in Cologne. The bank clerk had not been called up because he had a bad chest. He liked his cigarettes though and I gave him one of mine, which I used to buy from our canteen. They were American cigarettes if I remember, called Piedmont, and the German chap said that he liked them. He asked me if I could buy him some as he said that they were

*The victory parade, 1918. George Street, Pocklington.*

far better than the German ones. I thought for a while and didn't see any harm in getting a packet or two for him. I charged him double the price so I got mine free! The old man of the house used to grow his own tobacco and when he started to smoke it, he used to stink the place out. It was putrid! For coffee they used to roast barley, which added to the smell, and was a poor substitute.

I enjoyed my time in the army of occupation very much and it was an honour to be an officer's servant. I used to get a pass to go to Cologne now and again where I visited the cathedral, which was very beautiful. On one of my trips I bought a fiddle from a music shop. It was a very good one and was very cheap. I had learned to play a little before I joined the army and used to play with my dad and my brother Bob. I was only seventeen when I started. My father had kept pestering me to start playing and used to say that you weren't a Harrison unless you could play. I said to myself that I would show them, so I borrowed a fiddle from a friend and bought a tutor book by Henry Farmer for 1/6d and a music stand that cost the same. At nights I used to practice in our parlour with a candle for light as there was no electricity laid on. Of course we had two hang-up paraffin lamps, for the front room and living room, which were made of brass and were beautiful. I had learned to read music at school so I persevered and was soon able to play hymns and songs.

Now as time went by, getting near to March, my father applied to the authorities asking if I could be released from the army, which you could do if you were in business. My papers came through and I was demobbed in the second week of March 1919. It was a sad day when I left Germany and Lieutenant Horton wept when we said goodbye. I said cheerio to my mate Cox and a few other pals and went to Cologne where I embarked on a steamer and sailed down the Rhine to Rotterdam. It was a quiet, pleasant trip down river, but quite different when we got into the harbour and saw the tugs bobbing up and down like corks. I thought to myself if the sea is as rough as that in the harbour, what will it be like on the open sea? I soon found out; the minute we left the shore the boat began to rock as we bumped into a March gale. It blew, rained and snowed and I never thought we would make it. A March gale is bad enough on land, but it is much worse at sea; how the hell that boat rode the waves, I don't know! I was as sick as a dog and got wet through as the mountainous seas broke over the ship. We passed a Belgian relief boat that was taking refugees back to Belgium from Britain.

Anyway we got home and docked at Harwich; wasn't I pleased to get off that boat onto dry land? We lined up on the quay, soaking wet and freezing. There somebody brought us two paper bags, one with sausage rolls and the other with sandwiches and buns which were very acceptable. I was so hungry I could have eaten a horse! We were then put on a train which took us to a camp at Clipstone, arriving at about one in the morning and it was about seven when I finally left the army. All the time we were in our wet clothes with no fires to dry us out and we had to wait until we got home; that was how we were treated, but getting home was what mattered. I travelled on the train with a sergeant as far as York, where I got the train to Nunburnholme Station, which was in fact in the next village at Burnby, and from there I walked home.

# Catch Work in the 1920s

I want to say a few words about a friend of mine called Charlie Richardson who came to live with his uncle at Nunburnholme, on a small holding, as his uncle was getting on a bit. When he wasn't working for his uncle, he used to do a bit of catch work which means helping other farmers with such jobs as hoeing turnips and carrying corn on threshing days and such like. I was pleased to be home with a good bed to sleep in and good food to eat. I had a job in the winter feeding the threshing machine for my father, but I had to do catch work in the summer, until I got my job back at Warter.

Charlie and I got work on the Warter estate for the summer and our first job was mowing thistles with a scythe or 'lay', as we used to call it. If a field of corn had a lot of thistles in it, the farmer used to get his men to cut them from the ground which was called 'looking'. Now all this is finished as sprays are used and you don't see thistles in corn fields any more. We had to mow thistles in a field called the Park which was about a hundred acres and I never saw as many thistles in my life. It was just like mowing corn.

After we finished we went hoeing turnips and then made hay. We didn't stop for harvest, as Charlie had to be back helping his uncle with the harvest and I had to be back with my father getting the threshing machine, straw elevator and straw trasser ready for the season. During the winter months we used to go from farm to farm threshing the farmers' corn. My father drove the Fowler traction engine and I used to feed the machine. A chap called Tommy Nichols cut the band that was tied round the sheaves. We were kept in work all through the winter. It was a dirty job, what with the dust from the straw and the smoke from the engine. Another hazard we had to face were thistles in the corn sheaves.

In 1920 I went to work on the estate at Warter again, but I was on my own as Charlie couldn't go, due to pressure of work on his uncle's farm. I was sent to mow thistles in the same field but there weren't as many this time. After finishing this I went hoeing turnips at Skygate farm, where Mr George Elsworth was the foreman at the time. He had a son called George who worked with me at Warter when I started working there again. His daughter, Mary, was a good pianist.

One day when the other men and I were hoeing in the field, a storm developed and there was no shelter from the rain apart from a few trees and naturally we picked the one with the most branches. I thought I'd give my hoe a sharpen with a file. There was a flash and a crack and my file flew out of my hand. My arm was numb and I daren't look down at it, but after a while the blood began to circulate. I had been struck by lightning and was thankful that I was no worse. One of the chaps shouted,

"Leave the bloody file alone, you'll have us all killed!"

Anyway, that taught me a lesson!

Believe it or not that wasn't the only time I got struck by lightning. Once I was struck riding my bicycle up Featherbed Lane, which goes from Nunburnholme to Kilnwick Percy.

I then got a job at Garforth Farm which Sam Featherstone farmed with his sons, Tom and Charlie, together with Walt Jobson, who lived in Nunburnholme. Sam Featherstone was in the village and happened to see my Dad and told him that he was seeking men to hoe turnips and my Dad shouted for me. Mr Featherstone asked me if I would come and hoe turnips, which I agreed to do. So next morning, I got to the farm at seven in the morning but the men were already in the field. When I got to the field, Charlie pointed out my hoe and file which were leaning against the hedge and I set about hoeing ten rows. This was called break hoeing. That first half day nobody spoke to me, which I thought was a bit tame, so I decided to get the conversation going. In the afternoon Mr Featherstone came into the field to see what sort of a job I was making and told me that I could hoe turnips well. He also told me not to take any notice of 'those silly buggers' in the field.

We were finishing this hoeing when Dicky Wood, who farmed Methill Hall, next to Garforth Farm asked me if I would come and hoe some turnips for him. I agreed to this and started at eight the next morning; notice the difference the two farmers started. After this job, I went back to Garforth Farm to help with the harvest. Because the corn was not yet ready, I mowed a field of grass that was full of thistles for which I was paid £2.10s which was good pay at this time. I got there in my own time and came home in my own time and Mr Featherstone was satisfied as long as I got those thistles mown.

In those days you were engaged for a month at harvest and if it rained we had other jobs to do such as mending bags with a curved 'poke needle' and binder twine for thread. Other jobs were cleaning out horse boxes and chucking the manure out into the fold yard. We had to whitewash the walls of the buildings and 'muck plugging', which was filling carts with manure out of the fold yard which would be spread on the land. If it was a dewy morning you went to draw straw from the year before's wheat-straw stack to thatch the new corn stacks. As time went by, we got the harvest in, I was paid and Mr Featherstone asked me to come back next year. I said that I would if I had not got a job already but jobs weren't easy to get. I used to meet Charlie and Tom Featherstone, the farmer's sons, in the Oddfellow's Arms in Pocklinghton every Saturday night.

I did go back to work for the Featherstones in the next year, hoeing turnips and harvesting. A chap called Ernie Hall, who also came from Nunburnholme and whom I got on well with, was also working there. One morning we were asked to go into a field of oats again next to a wood called ' Meerbalks' and start opening it out. The farmer asked Ernie to mow and me to tie up the corn into sheaves. I had to gather up the corn with a rake which had three prongs or tines. Each tine was about six inches long and there was about three inches between them. This kind of rake was also used on threshing days for raking the 'caff' (chaff) into a sheet to be carried away. The reason for 'opening out' the field was to make room for the binder which was a kind of reaping machine which cut the corn, tied it up and threw out the sheaves. This machine was pulled by horses or a tractor. Well we got started and after a while I noticed that Ernie wasn't making a very good job.

"Bloody scythe's no good!" he said and asked me if I would try it. I got hold of the scythe, turned my back on him and started to sharpen it. I kept talking to him so that he couldn't see how I did it and then started to mow. I took a bigger break because I was longer in the arm than Ernie. At that moment Mr Featherstone came to see how we were getting on and asked why we'd changed over. Ernie said that I could beat him at mowing and Mr Featherstone said that I was a bit of a dark horse. What they didn't know was that I had learned to mow grass in Warter Priory gardens and was taught by an old hand called William Frankish. Ernie would have done better if he had sharpened the scythe properly. The right way to do this is to use the stone or 'strickle' as we called it, the full length of the blade, from the heel to the point; Ernie wasn't doing it like this but in short strokes which is wrong as you can take the cutting edge off the blade.

When the harvest was over the threshing season came and I took up my winter job which was feeding sheaves for my father on his rounds of the farms. I was occupied all winter doing this and in the summer I got my old job back in Warter Priory gardens. I worked there until the autumn when I rejoined my father. I got no wages when working for my father, as that was the way of life at that time; duty to your parents.

# Home made music

*Bill loved music all his life and the next section of his story goes on to describe some of these activities from 1919 to 1942. His father, Harry, played fiddle for dances and "wasn't a bad hand", according to Bill. Besides playing for dances, musicians used to play in the church and were a major feature of Christmas festivities. Not everybody appeared to enjoy the home-made music, however, as this excerpt from "Yorkshire Reminiscences", written by the Reverend Marmaduke Morris in 1922 suggests:*

*"When my father (F.O. Morris) went to Nunburnholme, there were a number of "musicianers" as they were called, who played various instruments in church every Sunday. I do not fancy that the sounds they played were particularly harmonious; at all events, they were soon suppressed and a harmonium procured...*

*Men used to come round in the early hours of the morning singing hymns of various kinds and some of the selections were by no means appropriate to the season and my sister once suggested that "Art thou languid" was not quite the thing for Christmas to which one of the songsters replied,*

*"Ah reckon nowt aboot t' wo'ds. It soons weel of a neet.""*

*Although, as Morris writes, the "musicianers" no longer played in the church, they continued playing carols in the streets in Bill's time. Could one of them have been Bill's father? Bill's own description contrasts greatly with that of Morris.*

I will leave off writing about work and tell you about my musical and singing career. I learned music with being in the church choir and at school in Nunburnholme. The Harrison family were all musical in various ways, either playing or singing, so you see it was a gift I was born with, I used it in the best way possible, but it was only a side line because we had to work to live. I taught myself to play the cello, bought an instruction book to help me sort out the fingering and bowing. I progressed well, getting to read the bass clef well. I mentioned earlier that I had learned to play hymns and songs on the violin before I was called up in 1917 and that I bought a violin when I was with the army of occupation in Cologne. I was a fool for selling that fiddle to a chap before I left Germany; but that's history.

My brother, father and me used to go Christmas singing. My father and Bob played fiddles and I played an old cello which had an

*Bill with violin aged 21.*

*Bob Harrison.*

iron bar in the neck to keep it straight. With the stand out full-length, I could play the cello standing up. We used to go in a trap to Burnby and Hayton and play there.

On Christmas Day itself, we played in the street at Nunburnholme, starting up at the bottom end against the church. We were asked into every house where we were given mince pies, apple pies and pork pie. Most people used to keep a pig in those days, which they would kill just before Christmas. We had a drink as well and by the time we'd finished we were fit to burst. Everybody enjoyed it, it was grand.

[*Among Bill's recollections recorded by Jim Eldon was this story about Bill and his father playing at Kilnwick Percy Hall:*]

"We went up to Kilnwick Percy Hall in Captain Whittle's time. We weren't invited, we just used to go. If nobody went they used to grumble:
"We've had no singers nor nowt!"
Once we were playing carols at Kilnwick and were in the Butler's pantry having something to eat and drink...the big curtains parted all the way, so we struck up with "While Shepherd's", father taking the lead, my brother playing parts and I played bass. Captain Whittle gave us two quid!. He was Master of the Foxhounds so I said to my dad,
"John Peel."
When we started the Captain took his son, a school lad who had his sailor suit on and started hopping, gallop, round the table — and we got another couple of quid!"]

My first engagement playing the cello was with Harry Hotham's dance band in the Victoria Hall, Pocklington for the Peace Ball in 1919.

After I was demobbed and got settled down to civilian life, I went to Sidney Gray who was a well known Pocklington violinist and had ten lessons. My brother Bob was a good player and was a member of R.D. Gray's dance band. He told Mr Gray that I could play and read music so Mr Gray asked him to bring me along the next time he had an engagement, which was at Elvington village hall, an ex-army hut. I thought playing with a dance band was great and as time went by, I improved my cello playing and started playing that in the band instead of the violin, as Mr Gray thought that would be a better combination. I did this for two years, until my brother Bob left to join Harry Hotham's dance band, which meant that I had to take up the violin again. I had kept up my playing and Mr Gray thought I was a better reader than Bob, also a better time-keeper.

We were kept busy all winter, playing for dances at the Masonic halls at Pocklington, Driffield, Malton and the church hall at Sherburn in Elmet, besides playing in the villages around and about. The band consisted of Mr Gray, who was a self-employed saddler, on the piano, Neville Todd, who worked in a tailor's shop, played the drums but was eventually replaced by Joe Lamb, a jeweller from Railway Street, Pocklington, when Neville went to work in Leeds. Another member of the band was Ernie Shepherdson from Barmby Moor, who played the Ströh fiddle, which was a fiddle with a horn like a gramophone. When we played at Sherburn, we stayed the night at the Red Bay hotel and caught the train in the morning. Then I cycled home to Nunburnholme. It was tiring, but I loved it.

We used to have dances in the school at Nunburnholme. There were two grate holes in the floor which were a bit higher than the floor and when you waltzed, you would catch your dance shoes in them and turn over end. Sally Frear taught me how to dance. She was a big woman and must have weighed about sixteen stone, but was very light on her feet. She used to grab you in the middle of the back and you were on her stomach all the time, sometimes with your feet off the ground!

Mr Gray left the band when he joined the Freemasons and a young lad called Harold Flint took over on piano. Joe Lamb also packed in when Mr Gray finished and George Coulson took his place. Harold's brother George who played the cornet also joined and we renamed the band 'The Modern Dance Band'. We were together for quite a long time and then Harold Flint left to take up a post up north together with his brother. Well the band broke up. I often wonder how I did it, as many a time I got home at four in the morning, gone to bed and got up half an hour later, leaping on my bike to go to get the traction engine steamed up for a day's threshing. I would then feed the machine all day, come home, get dressed up and then go out again. Before the band broke up, another friend of mine, Eric Towle joined to play piano. His son Brian also came along to play clarinet or saxophone, I just forget which. Both father and son were fine musicians. I played with many pianists in my time: Bert Buttle, R.D. Gray, Harry Hotham, Bernard Hotham, Miss E. Thompson, Eric Towle, Harold Flint,

*May festivities in Nunburnholme behind Wold View, c.1929. Bill and family played for the dance which was organised by Mrs. Newlove who then taught at the school.*

Miss M. Thomas, Miss J. Barker, Miss Aldred and my sister Doris, who at the time I am writing, still lives in Nafferton aged 89.

Bert Buttle formed a male voice choir and everybody who wanted to join had to have a voice test, which consisted of singing a scale. When it came to my turn, I passed and I was immediately asked to sing lead tenor. The choir consisted of first tenors, second tenors, baritones and basses. I still continued my fiddle playing at dances. Once the choir had a singing engagement at Market Weighton and I couldn't go because I was dance playing. Mr Buttle was very upset but he knew about my other commitment. Anyway the choir went to Market Weighton and tragically Mr Buttle died that night while conducting the orchestra, so the choir broke up. It was a sad occasion and I was very upset.

After a while, Mr Eric Towle sent out invitations to members of the choir with a view to forming a new choir, so we got back together again with Mr Towle as conductor. Some of the old members retired and new members joined. We got a lot of bookings and I played solo violin with the choir at concerts. We had a great time. It was fine comradeship. We sang at the Methodist churches at

Kirbymoorside, Pickering, York, Driffield, Pocklington and villages round about.

Mr Towle was a fine and talented musician who played the violin and piano and played the organ at the methodist chapel on Union Street, Pocklington, before it closed. He then became joint organist at the Methodist church in Chapmangate and conducted the circuit choir until he was taken ill and died. His death was a great loss to Pocklington and I felt privileged to be a member of his choir. We sang 'Messiah' at the church which was a great achievement. Mr Albert Sheen, a member of the male voice choir, took over as conductor of the male voice choir and is doing a very good job even now as I write this book. Good luck to you all, Albert and the lads. There was nothing I liked better than singing in a male voice choir or listening to one. Men's voices to me sounded like a church organ. I have liked all church music ever since I joined the choir at Nunburnholme church. Now I am 87 and not much good at singing; age beats everything.

# More catch work in the 1930s

*Although work was hard to come by at this time, Bill was lucky and being prepared to do practically anything, was never out of a job. He even took up an appointment as a male nurse in Cheshire. The threshing business was going through a difficult time due to the new technology in agriculture and family problems.*

I got to work hoeing turnips at Burnby Wold, which was farmed at the time by the Scotts, who also farmed at Hayton, and this farm was run by Willie Scott the son of Jimmy. After this I got back to work in Warter Priory Gardens for a little while, then I had to leave because I wasn't a footballer and they were forming a team, and anybody who could play football got a job in the gardens. I was at a loose end so I had a ride out on my bike to Hayton one day and called at the Plough Inn for a glass of beer. The Landlord was Tom Stabler and I told him about my losing the job at the gardens. He told me that the Rector of Burnby was looking for a man to tidy up his garden. The Rector was called the Reverend Booty and when I called to see him, he was delighted that I had called. He had a housekeeper called Ada Oxtoby who was a good sort and cooked me lunch twice a day. I used to fetch the Reverend cigarettes from the Post Office and help him to smoke them; you see he had known me since I was a boy, as he had been Vicar of Warter. One morning when I was coming to an end of tidying his garden he came to have a talk and said that a friend of his called George Wright, who had previously farmed at Grimthorpe, wanted a man for a few weeks, so I got work there for the summer. Brinkworth Hall was a nice gentleman's residence which was not too big. The gardener was called Turner and we got on very well. By that time I had a motor cycle, so I had no trouble getting to work. I started work at eight in the morning and finished at five for which I was paid 36s a week and my insurance stamp paid, petrol and oil for my motor bike and a jug of tea for my dinner, which wasn't bad for that time. I enjoyed working there but the time came for me to leave. Both Mr Wright and Turner were sorry to see me go and both thanked me for helping them. The day I left, Mr Wright came and shook my hand and said he would have liked to keep me on, as I had more knowledge of gardening than Turner, but he couldn't afford to keep us both on and I knew what he was thinking.

Winter passed and spring came and there was an advert in the press which read:

'Wanted. A man to train as a male nurse. Ability as a musician would be an advantage.'

Well I wrote off and was asked to go for an interview and got the job. I stayed the night at the home of my Uncle George and Aunt Hannah in Sale, Cheshire. The name of the institution was Calderstone and was not far from the small town of Whalley which is in Lancashire. The place consisted of different wards or blocks; a consumption ward an epileptic ward and G Block, commonly known as the farm block as this housed the patients who worked on the farm. My bedroom was in this block. I started work the day before Good Friday and my first day's duty was in the sports field at a football match. All the other nurses and myself were lined up round the field to prevent any of the inmates from absconding. This instutition was a mental hospital, it was big and had its own church and ballroom. I was settling down very well in my new career which was quite different from working in fields and gardens and playing in the orchestra was quite a treat, but my mother wrote asking me to come home, so I left.

I told my mother that I would stay with her as long as she lived, which I did. My father wasted his money and used to like his tipple until he got too old. He wasn't a bad sort really and we had a good table. The problems happened when he had too much to drink. He came back from Pocklington one day the worse for drink and started his tantrums. He shouted at me, calling me a whippersnapper. My mother got frightened and motioned to me to be quiet and say nothing, but I thought different, so I stood up to him and told him what I thought about him. He didn't like this and said that he would teach me a lesson. He got out of the chair and took a swipe at me and then fell over. He got onto his knees and stopped there as he was too drunk to do anything. It was a good job that it ended like that before any more damage was done. It taught him a lesson though and he respected me a lot more after that because I had stood up to him. In fact he gave me £10 to buy a new cycle which I had seen in Fox's cycle shop.

If I remember, the shop was where Eric Lee's electrical shop is now. This was in the early 1930's and my bike consisted of a 26 inch frame, 28 inch wheels, lever brakes, straight handle bars with curves at the end, mudguards and Sturmey Archer three speed gear with an oil-bath case. This meant that the gear wheel, chains and back wheel sprocket were running in oil. There was also a pump and an acetylene lamp which burned carbide. The bottom of this lamp fitted onto slots or grooves where you put the carbide. In the top part of the lamp was the water chamber with a lever at the top of it. When you turned the lever left it allowed the water to drop onto the carbide which caused a gas. In the front part of the lamp was a burner, either a single or double one. The gas came through the burner and then you lit it. This produced a very good light and you had to use your judgement as to the amount of water you allowed to drop onto the carbide. With this bike I got a saddlebag filled with spanners and tools, as well as a tin of solution and patches for mending punctures. All this came to £7 if you paid cash which I did. This bike hadn't a bright patch on it and was enamelled black and gold. I think it was made by a firm from Barton-on-Humber and the name of the bike was a 'Hercules'. I think the name of the firm was Hopper. It was a good strong bike.

I was still at a loose end doing catch jobs and did some gardening for the vicar of Nunburnholme, the Reverend Stott. One morning when I was thinning out a shrubbery he came out to have a chat, smoking his pipe. He suddenly asked me:

"How do you like my new pipe, William?"

Well I told him it looked a nice one and he replied that he had got it from York station,

"I think I will give you it," he continued and he did.

He would come out sometimes, just before mid-day and ask me to bring my violin into the vicarage. That meant that there was no gardening done that afternoon. He was a good pianist who could play a bit of anything. Eventually he retired and moved up to Scarborough so I was out of a job again; work wasn't very plentiful in the early 'Thirties and I was luckier than a lot of chaps as I had my dance playing to fall back on, so I was never short of a bob or two. I think I only had my insurance card franked twice in my working life. I would have a go at anything as there wasn't much choice at the time. I have known chaps that were out of work in the district who were forced to go bush-beating on the Warter estate. The head keeper or estate manager would go down to the labour exchange at Pocklington to see how many men were out of work. It was just the same if a farmer wanted men for threshing. In those days there was a fair bit of 'Jack strawing', that was carrying loose straw from the

*Bill's male voice quartet. Joe Johnson and Billy (back), Eric Gray and Ted Wox.*

machine and if a chap wasn't used to carrying straw it was hard work; I have done a bit of it myself. I hoed turnips at Marginson's, in Kilnwick Percy, and have also weeded carrots on my knees, parting the rubbish from the young plants. This was a lousy job and you had to tie bags round your knees to keep them from getting sore from the thistles and nettles. At Scott's at Hayton, where I also harvested, my job was to take a cart to the harvest field. A chap called Tom Howden, was the forker who forked the sheaves from the stook onto the cart. I had never loaded sheaves onto a cart so I said to him:

"Tom, Thoo esty loaden cart and I etty fork them."

Well he champed and cussed and put a good load on; it was wheat that we were leading and I had only one rope to keep the sheaves on the cart. Coming across the headland the load pigged and the rear end of the load of sheaves dropped off. It was all high road leading. A farmer called Cliff Bland, who farmed near Hayton church was leading corn with his men and as I passed them, they were laughing like hell at my load. As I got nearer to the stack yard I could see Willie Scott and his men bursting with laughter and when I got into the yard, the first thing they said was:

"Thoo's been loading!"

I answered that I hadn't but that I would load the next load. Well I got teamed and went back to the field and told Tom what had happened. He stamped and raved again and I told him that if I had used two ropes instead of one, the load would have carried and insisted that I would load the next one. He asked me if I had loaded before and he started to fork and I started to load. He kept saying that I had to put them this way and that, but I ignored him and squared the cross sheaves to make a good foundation about two feet high at each side and I eventually got a good load on the cart and brought them to the stackyard without spilling a single sheaf. It was a queerish load, but I improved as I went on.

The horse I had pulling the cart was short, fat and called Cobby. Tom Oxtoby had him before I took him over and he warned me to watch the high road as the horse didn't like steam wagons. Me and the horse got on famously. He was a bit frisky, but I talked to him. You want to treat animals like human beings if it's possible and I had a brain wave and bought some sugar at Nunburnholme shop and filled my pockets. The next day, every time we met a steam wagon I gave him a lump of sugar which quietened him down. When old Tom asked me how I had got on with the horse, I told him

*Harry Harrison and threshing set. Bill's father is standing on the traction engine.*

that I had had no bother at all with the sugar. I enjoyed taking the cart to the harvest field and loading sheaves as it was far better than throwing the sheaves to the man on the stack. There is a lot of skill in making a stack, especially topping it up to make it waterproof.

I was sorry when we had finished harvesting. I had got quite attached to the horse, Cobby and we were good friends. I didn't do any more catch-work after harvest but helped my dad get the threshing machine ready for the season. The straw elevator also had to be checked to see if it wanted any new links in the chain and there was the straw tier to fix. This machine was fixed onto the straw-end of the threshing machine, driven by a link chain from a cog wheel fixed onto the crank-shaft of the straw shaker. The straw dropped into a hopper on the straw tier and then it was tied in what we called a bottle of straw with binder twine. The weight of the bottle of straw released a lever and was thrown out by three prongs. The straw tier or 'trusser' as it was called was similar to a binder that cut the corn and threw out the sheaves. Another machine we used was called a knotter which tied a knot on the binder twine round the bottle of straw and the sheaves of corn. There was also a small knife which cut the binder twine; the weight of the bottle of straw from the trusser cut the binder twine and released the bottle of straw as it was thrown out.

It got round to 1936 and all the talk was about harvesting the American way, which meant that threshing machines would soon be out of date, though one or two farmers kept to the old-fashioned ways. There was no future in threshing for a living, so my father, who was getting on, sold the threshing machine, straw elevator and straw tier, and the traction engine went for scrap. If we had known then what we know now the whole threshing set would have made a lot of money.


### The Warter Priory Shoot

*In those days most large estates had a shoot and Warter Priory was no exception. The writer of the "Hull Times" article on the estate describes viewing the shooting book and records the following entries, chosen at random:*

*"23-10-1923 Guns: Duke of Roxburgh, Duke of Sutherland, Lord Blandford, Lord Weymess, Lord Dalmeny, Sir Matthew Wilson, Colonel Claude Willoughby, Captain H. De Trafford, Colonel Guy Wilson.*

*Total: 1,069 head.*

*10th, 11th, 12th, December 1924, Guns: Duke of Roxburgh, Lord Londonderry, Lord Blandford, Lord Lovat, Lord Dalmeny, Captain Boyd Rochfort and Colonel Guy Wilson.*

*Total for three days: 3,424.*

*...In connection with these shoots it should be added that after the requirements of the participators have been satiated and a quantity has been dispatched to Lady Nunburnholme's personal friends the remainder is sent to, or sold for charitable institutions. The coverts at Warter are beyond compare and all the trees are superb."*

*The shoot continued after the Warter Estate was sold to Mr George Vestey in 1929 and Bill describes what one of the shoots was like for one of the more humble participators, casting rather a different perspective on the proceedings.*

I was asked to go back to work at the Priory full time and what with my gardening and dance playing, I was doing very well. The Honourable George Vestey bought the estate in 1929 and kept the gardens going, opening them to the public every summer. It was a pleasure for us gardeners to see people walking about, asking questions about the names of the plants and how to grow them.

In the winter, four or five of us pleasure-ground gardeners used to go bush beating which was quite a change. We weren't allowed to smoke whilst working in the gardens so it was quite a change to have a quick drag when we were driving the game up to the gentry waiting to shoot. The game included pheasants, partridges, hares, rabbits, woodcock and pigeons. Tom England was the head-keeper and his father, Ben, who was head-keeper before him used to go loading. Every gentleman would have to have a man to carry the guns and cartridges and after every stand the game cart used to meet you, and the man on this would ask you if you wanted the cartridge bag filling up. The driver was called Bill Berriman. He had a dry sense of humour but was always pleasant and would share a joke with you.

Each gentleman had two guns and the job of the loader was to put the cartridges into the gun and hand it back. The gentleman might hand you the empty gun with his left or right hand and you had to be quick at the job, especially if the pheasants were flying over in numbers. We were driving the game out at one shoot, when Tom, the head-keeper came up the line and stopped in front of me saying:

"Bill, can you loaden?"

"Yes," I replied.

"Go to Mr Storey because my ord man's buggered."

This was the second drive and there had been a keen frost the night before and Tom's father couldn't walk on rough and ploughed land as his feet hurt him too much. Now Mr Storey was the estate agent and he used to make the number up if a gentleman couldn't get. He once told me that he was going hunting with the fox-hounds the same day there was a shoot on. Well anyway, a gentleman dropped out and Mr Storey had to cancel his hunting in order to fill in; he was a bit annoyed about this, but was friendly enough to get on with, so we talked about cricket and gardening.

A three day shoot used to held at Warter Priory which included Golden Valley, Silver Valley and High Cliffe. This was a big affair, with eight standing guns and the keepers had guns to shoot the hares that ran back through the beaters' line. In his heyday, Mr Vestey used to shoot with three guns and his loaders were Sid Slater, who was his chauffeur and Jack Vaughan, a keeper from another estate. Thursday, Friday and Saturday used to be the days for the big shoot at that time and one Wednesday, when I was working in the

Gardens, word came from the head-keeper that I had to load for a Mr Johnson, a big fellow well over six feet with a brother the same size. I had to be at the Priory by half-past eight on the Thursday morning and I went to the old laundry where all the gentlemen's guns and cartridges were stored. I saw Mr Johnson's brother's chauffeur putting his boss's guns together. They would bring their guns in a case and you had to fit them together and then place them in a canvas bag and carry them to the shoot. When I went in I told the loader that I had come to load for Mr Johnson. He showed me where Mr Johnson's guns were, I fitted them together and put them into their canvas bags and Mr Johnson's brother's loader asked me how many cartridges we would need to take. I told him that we would need five hundred for a start and he gave me a stare and said that I must be joking. I told him that he would soon find out! The gentry used to fire when the game was too far off and would have a go at anything chancing their luck. They used to buy them in bulk and each one used to cost about a penny in those days.

# Marriage and Lyndhurst

At that time there was an under estate manager called Mr Hughes who played the violin and we soon got together to form a trio with Miss Madge Thomas on piano. We used to play at Sixpenny Hops in the servants' hall at Warter Priory once a week during the winter months and sometimes at dances in Warter school. My late wife's sister, Agnes, was a very good dancer, especially at the old time waltz. I also danced with Miss Lily Forth and Miss Florrie Coulson.

About this time I started courting my late wife Edna, daughter of James Southcote who lived in George Street, Pocklington, and had a bit of land on which he had a few cows before he built a house down Barmby road, just over the railway crossing as it was then. He used to buy carrots and clean them for the gentry in Lincolnshire and one of these gentlemen made him a present of a pipe and case, which I have still got. I mentioned before that I had promised to stay with my mother as long as she lived. She died on 21st March 1938. After my father packed up threshing, he worked for Percy Moore, a farmer at Throstle Nest, near Pocklington, driving a tractor, after which he moved on to work at Nunburnholme vicarage keeping the place tidy and looking after the machine that provided light for the vicarage, before electricity was laid on in the village. My niece, Celia, looked after my father and me after my mother died.

One day I was talking to George Noble, the estate plumber, when he told me that Billy Mennell, Mr Tom English's gardener had died and he thought that it would be a good job to take on. Mr English lived at Lyndhurst, Pocklington, and I decided to see him about the job. I plucked up courage and knocked on the back door. A maid opened it and I asked if I could see Mr English. She went back into the house and came back a few minutes later and told me that he would see me, so she led me into the drawing room.

"Now young man, what can I do for you?" he asked.

I answered that I had come to apply for the post of gardener and told him that I was Harry Harrison's son from Nunburnholme. He said that he knew my father well, as he bought corn from a farmer whom my father threshed for. He asked me if I was working and I told him that I was at Warter Priory gardens. Mr English asked me why I wanted to leave and I answered that I wanted a change and that I had two good references, one from the head gardener, Mr W. Kitching, and the other from the Reverend Booty, the rector of

Burnby. I asked him if he wanted to see them but he answered that my name was enough for him. He said he would pay me £2.00 per week and pay my insurance stamp, plus anything I grew in the garden and even kindling for lighting the fire. He offered me a bottle of beer and I thanked him very much. We carried on talking and he told me that he had another young man working for him who had been there for some time called Wilfred Gray. Mr English said that he would have a word with Gray and warned me that he might be a bit jealous, but that was something that we had to work out. Mr English then asked me how old I was and I told him that I was forty.

"That's just the right age," he answered, "You can take charge of the place as Gray is far too young. By the way, what is your christian name?"

I told him that it was William and he exclaimed that his name was William also and that his previous gardener, Mennell had the same name. The English family always called me Harrison though.

I was sorry to leave my old job in one sense as I missed all my mates there, but I decided that I had to branch out. One of my mates, Jim Patrick, gave me a very good kitchen garden book which proved very valuable and I gave him five shillings for it. This book was written by Edwin Beckett from Aldenham House gardens at Elstree, Herts. and was published in 1927. In my opinion it is as good as any modern gardening book.

I was a bit nervous when Monday morning came round as I had been used to doing as I was told and now I had to take charge of the place. I cycled from Nunburnholme arriving at Lyndhurst, where I met Wilfred Gray and shook hands with him. He showed me round the place. There was an old lean-to greenhouse which had seen better days and I told Wilfred that Mr English would have to buy a new one. The garden tools were worn out and the cold-frames for planting out needed repairing but the orchard was one of the best in Pocklington and may have been planned out by a green-grocer called James Johnson, who used to have a shop on George Street.

Despite what Mr English had said, Wilfred and I got on very well and he was glad that I had come to take over. Mr English was a big shooting man having shooting rights from Millington Wood to his brother's estate at Yapham, as well as Little Givendale. He once bought Wilfred and me a pair of boots each from Stead and Simpson's shop in Market Place, Pocklington and we picked ones called "Dreadnoughts" which had strong leather soles and were

*Billy working at Warter Priory in the 1930s.*

*Lyndhurst.*

heavy and well nailed. All this happened in 1938 and we had plenty to do what with pruning fruit trees, digging and getting the garden ready for planting in the Spring.

1939 came round and Edna thought that it was about time that we were wed. That made me do a lot of thinking; it was alright getting married but where were we going to live? We had a bit of luck as we were offered a cottage that belonged to Mr Ernest Smith, a joiner and undertaker who lived in Union Street, which was adjoining his yard. When we went to look at it, a mate of mine George Coulson was decorating it. It was a two bedroom cottage with a gas cooker and lighting, so we said that it would suit us very much and we agreed on a rent of 5s.6d per week.

We were married on Easter Saturday, 8th April 1939, by the Rev. Hunt in Pocklington parish church. Everything went very well. We didn't splash out in a big way but invited a few friends round for a few drinks and a meal at my wife's father's.

We went to Bridlington for the weekend and stayed with my wife's cousin Mabel; I had to be back on the Easter Monday because I was playing at a dance in the Victoria Hall, Pocklington.

I bought some furniture for the house from my landlord, such as a bedroom suite which I have got still and second-hand carpets but it was all good stuff. We came home from our short honeymoon at about tea-time.

Starting a home of your own is a wonderful experience. As we approached our house we saw that the chimney was reeking smoke and I asked my wife who could have lit the fire. We had no occasion to unlock the front door as it was already open. We walked straight in and found that every bit of furniture and all the carpets had been put in the right place as our landlord Ernest Smith had been in to see to it. I asked him how much he wanted for doing it and he replied, nothing; even the kettle was boiling on the hob and the table was set. Nobody could have had a better landlord and landlady than the Smiths. All I did was put down the stair-carpet!

My social life was good in Pocklington and I was asked by Wilf Gray to join the brass band; I had never blown a brass instrument in my life and I thought that 40 was a bit old for starting. Anyway, I agreed and Wilf bought me a three valve trombone to practice on which was patched up with sticking plaster, and I got to play it fairly well. As there were two trombonists in the band already, the conductor, Jim Wilson, asked me if I'd like to have a go on the tenor horn, which I agreed to have a go at. I had two other changes of instrument, first the euphonium and then the E-flat Bass which I liked best. They were happy days.

One day I was approached by Sergeant David Etherington and asked if I would join the special constables, and I said yes. One of our duties was to move cars on if they were parked near a bridge or a gateway. It was summer and a special constable called Harry Moore and I were on duty one night patrolling the road from the bottom of the Green, to the high road, to South Moor House, when we saw one car parked on a small bridge. My mate Harry said it was dangerous to approach a car. I said it was our duty to move them on, so I decided, as I was bigger than my mate, I would do the job. So off I went, wearing my uniform with its police cap, cape and truncheon and when I looked into the car, I saw a couple on the back seat having a good time! They were nearly naked and you ought to have seen their faces when I tapped on the window and showed them my warrant card. I told them that they weren't allowed to park in gateways or near bridges and gave them five minutes to get on their way. When I told my mate what had happened, he said,

"To think what I have missed!"

September came and England declared war on Germany on Sunday, 3rd September. On that day I happened to be at my old friend Joe Johnson's house in Victoria road. My mate Wilf Gray was called up to join the army, so I was by myself in the gardens at Lyndhurst. I think I am right in saying that Wilf was killed on active service.

That reminded me of when I served in the First World War, but I was one of the lucky ones.

One morning when I was cleaning Mr English's shoes in the saddle house, he came out to have a chat and said that he had bought another house, the manor house at Millington and asked me if I would go with him. I said that I would have to consult with my wife. She agreed. I said that Millington was near enough to travel from Pocklington every day. But Mr English told me that he had bought the old chapel as well and said that he would make it into a house for us. We planned where to have the garden, a lawn and a place to plant fruit trees and a few shrubs. I had a hell of a lot of work to do as the place was nearly all grass before.

I used to cycle from Pocklington everyday. I planted fifteen apple trees, two cherry trees and an Austrian pine as well as other shrubs and a hedge of mixed privet and thorn. Then I started digging a garden from grass; it was hard work but I was a fit man and enjoyed creating something. Then there was the lawn to make and new paths to lay. Mrs Booth lived at the manor at that time and I used to chop her a few sticks and post her mail. It took me quite a while to make the place something to look at.

I shall always remember one Sunday night; me and my wife were reading by the fireside at about six, when I heard a plane flying over Pocklington. I said to my wife,

"That's Jerry."

When my wife asked me how I knew, I told her that I recognised it by the hum. Without putting my hat on I went straight across the street to talk to three or four chaps who were standing by Herbert Buttle's cobblers shop. I told them that I had heard the plane. By that time it had dropped about sixteen bombs on Garth Ends. A woman called Miss Young was killed and two pieces of shrapnel fell very close to us chaps standing on the pavement. This incident happened on 10th November 1940.

## Millington

Mr and Mrs English left Lyndhurst and moved to Millington on 2nd March, 1941. I was sorry to leave as the garden was such a pleasant one to work in and the soil was so good it would grow anything. What a difference when I started making a garden at the Manor among chalk soil. You couldn't use a spade for digging as there was too much chalk. I had to use a potato fork which had flat tines or a square tined fork. There was one good thing, I had plenty of manure and fertiliser to put on the soil. Millington soil grew good peas and vegetables and the flavour was good. An old saying claimed that a swede turnip tasted better from the chalk than from a sand or gravel soil. I think that this is true as I have eaten swedes from many different types of soil and they were definitely better from the chalk.

As time went by I got the garden into shape. 1942 came and my daughter Bridget was born at her grandad's, James Southcote, at Field House, Barmby Road on March 15th. I was born at Nunburnholme on 15th July 1898 and my father's birthday was on 15th May.

We left Pocklington and came to live at the old chapel at Millington on Whit Monday 1942. I was sorry to leave the cottage in Union Street and the landlord, Ernest Smith, was also sorry we were leaving. It was better for me as I hadn't to bike from Pocklington every morning and in time we got settled down and got to know a few people. My neighbour was Mr Clark Nesom and I had only been living in the village a few days when he came round, shook me by the hand and wished me good luck. I got to know the family better as time went on. I wasn't a stranger to the village as I already knew Jim, Jack, Joe and Ernest Brown, George Foster, Ted Harness, George, Tom and Stanley Berriman and Dick Sterricer. There was also Jack Otley, Fred Roe and Bob Stephenson.

I was still a special constable when I came to Millington but after a while I was asked to stand down as there were already two special constables in the village. I was approached by Captain Ted Munby, a farmer from Huggate, about joining the Home Guard. After wearing a blue uniform I had to wear khaki. I never thought that I would have to wear khaki or fire a rifle again. It reminded me of the First World war which I took part in as a private in 2nd/6th West Yorkshires, in a battalion that was part of the 62nd, or 'John Bull' Division as it was called then. I liked being in the Home Guard much better than being a specal constable as there was more variety. We went drilling, shooting and on manoeuvres and I was made a Lance Corporal. I didn't want the stripe but was obliged to take it. We had a weekend camping in Londesborough Park and went to Lockington on manoeuvres and to the big ranges at Strensal and Hornsea.

My social life in Millington was good and my neighbours, Mr Nesom and family, used to ask me and my wife to go into their home for a bit of singing. My wife Edna and I used to help out with the singing at the chapel anniversary. They were great days and it is sad to say all this is finished. People get older and die and times change but I am sorry to say, not for the better.

# Postscript

*Although Bill's book ends on a somewhat sombre note, this is by no means a true reflection of the pleasure he gave many people through his conversation and music. He continued to work as a gardener until he was in his early eighties and always remained young at heart and remarkably agile although suffering from arthritis. He was a regular visitor to the Gate Inn where he enjoyed the occasional half of mild in the company of the genial landlord, Mr Alan Moore and his family.*

*In 1985, Bill went into Leeds hospital for a small operation and was asked when he had last been in hospital:*

*"Why, 1918, during the Great War," was Bill's reply. The doctors and nurses were most surprised as Bill by no means showed his age.*

*Bill also continued to play for dancing until he was seventy-five though not in such a hectic way as he describes in the book. He even rejoined a revived Pocklington Male voice choir in his early eighties.*

*In 1980 I introduced Bill to Jim Eldon, the Hull based folk singer/fiddler, who specialises in collecting songs and tunes from older people in East Yorkshire. Bill featured on several of Jim's Radio Humberside programmes, "Portrait of a village fiddler" and "Home Made Music". Jim also recorded a tape to accompany an article in the "Musical Tradition" magazine entitled "Billy Harrison – Yorkshire Wolds Fiddler" (No 7, mid 1987).*

*In this, Bill recounted several stories about his music that he did not include in his book and I am most grateful to Jim for allowing me to use some of his material. Bill had a large repertoire of dance tunes, many of which he had learned from his fath'r who had also played for village dances. Here is one of them, transcribed by Sefton Cottom who also did much to encourage Bill in his music.*

## Bill's Father's Polka

As Bill described, he and his father and brother used to play carols at Christmas. Many villages had their own tunes for carols and Nunburnholme was no exception. The favourite was this version of "While Shepherds" and once again I am most grateful to Sefton Cottom for transcribing this tune and writing out the original parts as played by Billy and his family. I have especially fond memories of this version of the carol as on my annual Christmas Eve visit to Bill and Bridget, Bill used to ask me to sing the melody while he played the bass part on his cello.

## While Shepherds

93

Bill also composed his own tunes whilst gardening and was thrilled to see his notes written down. The parts were added by Sefton. These hymn tunes also reflect Bill's great love of choral music.

**Stand up, stand up for Jesus.**

As well as composing his own music, Bill even made his own instruments: one string fiddles. He made these out of an empty cigar box, a piece of cable wire and half a broom stick. It is surprising how good they sounded. I was most honoured to be given one of these by Bridget after Billy's death.

Bill always enjoyed sharing his music, even into the 1980s and when the Ebor Morris men came from York for their New Year and Summer dance-outs, he joined in tune sessions with 'Pikey' Holland, the team's musician and anyone else who had their instrument with them. On one occasion, whilst the Morris team were dancing in the street outside the pub, Bill captivated the people who remained inside with sets of tunes he had learned from 'Pikey', as well as his own!

As a young man, Bill had enjoyed playing in the family string quartet described earlier and always said that he would fancy

94

playing in one again. Thanks to the co-operation of the most talented folk musician, Nigel Chippindale, who tragically died aged twenty-nine in February 1986, and Jim Eldon, this ambition was achieved and the ensuing recording played on BBC Radio Humberside.

Bill continued to live at Manor Cottage, to which he had moved in 1942. In this simple but homely converted chapel, where he lived with his daughter Bridget, he remained a popular village character until he died peacefully at home after a short illness. His funeral was most moving and the small Norman church at Millington was full to capacity and many people stood.

The number of people present from so many walks of life was a real tribute to Bill's great personality. I am sure that his book will be a lasting memorial to him.

Peter Halkon